Praise for *Unfinished Business*

"*Unfinished Business* is a rich, wise, and powerful work that reminds us to be ever mindful of that which is truly important. By taking honest and courageous stock of his own unfinished business, Lee Kravitz calls on us all to live lives that honor our best selves. It is a timely and inspiring book."   **—Dave Isay, founder of StoryCorps**

"Self-effacing, self-aware, [Kravitz] embarks on a journey in which he reconnects with a schizophrenic aunt neglected by their family, forgives a high school nemesis and honors a forgotten promise to an underprivileged African boy. What could have turned into a self-congratulatory, Disneyesque odyssey becomes an occasion for real kindnesses and growing sensitivity."   *—Time*

"[Kravitz's] journeys . . . are truthful, generous and worthwhile. Through his experiences, he found meaning, an acceptance of life's absurdity and the insight that so much comes down to attitude and keeping the many threads of life thrumming."
—Kirkus Reviews

"When Lee Kravitz lost his job as editor-in-chief of *Parade* magazine, he decided to spend a year connecting all the dots his busy working life had left emotionally adrift, reaching out to grasp the hands and hearts of family members, friends, and mentors he had left behind. His adventures in outreach are moving, and quietly inspiring."   *—Barnes & Noble Review*

"Everyone complains about not having enough time—but what happens when we get it? Lee Kravitz used losing his job as a springboard to the human things he should have done. In so doing, he turned bad into bountiful. A great lesson for us all."
—Mitch Albom, author of
Tuesdays with Morrie* and *Have A Little Faith

"[Kravitz] uses this life-changing moment as an opportunity to take stock of his life . . . The lesson to be shared: 'Be mindful of what is most important, and act on it. The rewards will be immediate and lasting.'"   *—Cleveland Jewish News*

"Kravitz is a thoughtful writer, and his memoir reveals a delicate personal journey." —*Publishers Weekly*

"*Unfinished Business* is not just the story of how and why and when Lee Kravitz decided to tie up his loose ends, although all that is here. It's also about the extraordinary and unexpected events that unfold once he embarks on his journey toward completion. This is an uplifting and truly life-affirming book."
—**Hope Edelman, author of *Motherless Daughters* and *The Possibility of Everything***

"The book has an ecumenical, inclusive, joyful spirituality running like a current under a stream . . . Discovering how to love in daily life is the spiritual equivalent of scaling the Alps." —**100memoirs.com**

"What could have led to a downward spiral of regret and self-doubt instead turned out to be the beginning of a new outlook on life . . . Excellently handled by Kravitz's deft and engaging prose."
—*Dallas Morning News*

"Inspirational but never preachy, Kravitz's memoir reminds us of what really matters . . . and shows us how to begin searching for, and finding it." —*Hudson Valley News*

"It's the kind of reportage-cum-memoir that I love . . . I found it fascinating." —**Michael Ruhlman, author of *The Making of a Chef*, on Ruhlman.com**

"This book will strike a chord with those of us who feel we've left some things behind in the relentless pursuit of work and careers."
—*Republican* (**Springfield**)

"The stuff that life should be made of—re-thinking, redoing, reliving."
—**UrbanBaby.com**

"Kravitz's story about unfinished business, part of the human condition, is a cautionary tale for all of us." —*Christian Century*

"A refreshingly different kind of bucket list." —*Reader's Digest*

UNFINISHED BUSINESS

ONE MAN'S EXTRAORDINARY YEAR
OF TRYING TO DO THE
RIGHT THINGS

Lee Kravitz

BLOOMSBURY

New York   Berlin   London   Sydney

Copyright © 2010 by Lee Kravitz
Foreword copyright © 2011 by Gail Sheehy
Questions for Discussion copyright © 2011 by Lee Kravitz
Stories from Readers copyright © 2011 by Lee Kravitz
Unfinished Business Toolkit copyright © 2011 by Lee Kravitz

Published by Bloomsbury USA, New York

All papers used by Bloomsbury USA are natural, recyclable products made from
wood grown in well-managed forests. The manufacturing processes conform to
the environmental regulations of the country of origin.

Library of Congress Cataloging-in-Publication Data
Kravitz, Lee.
    Unfinished business : one man's extraordinary year of trying to do the right things / Lee
Kravitz. — 1st U.S. ed.
        p. cm.
    ISBN-13: 978-1-59691-675-3 (alk. paper hardcover)
    ISBN-10: 1-59691-675-3 (alk. paper hardcover)
    1. Kravitz, Lee.   2. Conduct of life.   3. Forgiveness.   4. Karma.   5. Interpersonal
relations.   6. Middle-aged men—United States—Biography.   7. Midlife crisis—United
States.   I. Title.
    CT275.K865A3 2010
    973.932092—dc22
    [B]
2009052463

First published by Bloomsbury USA in 2010
This paperback edition published in 2011

Paperback ISBN: 978-1-60819-463-6

1 3 5 7 9 10 8 6 4 2

Typeset by Westchester Book Group
Printed in the United States of America by Quad/Graphics, Fairfield, Pennsylvania

To my parents Harry and Phyllis, and to
Elizabeth, with love.

Contents

Foreword

LEE KRAVITZ LOVED his work. He lived it. It was not only his identity, it was his demon. Like many men in high-powered careers, his mind was almost always occupied by his work, even if his body was at home or on vacation.

Over the years that Lee Kravitz was my editor at *Parade* magazine, we often had tea and talked about how challenging it is to strike the right balance in our lives. He confided that his father, a workaholic, drove him to become a professional baseball player. When a high school injury shattered his father's dream, Lee blamed him for pushing him so hard and began creating his own vision of his future. "I reinvented myself at fifteen," Lee told me. "That was when I decided I wanted to write."

In our First Adulthood, the years between eighteen and fifty, the passages are quite predictable. And Kravitz, as an ambitious Boomer, proceeded from stage to stage in typical fashion. He was precocious in Pulling Up Roots and exploring an identity of his own. He used the Tryout Twenties to travel the world as a footloose freelance writer. And like many young Americans in the Age of Aquarius, he enjoyed a prolonged adolescence until he was thirty. Only after a shaky Age 30 Passage did he enter the Settling-Down stage, at thirty-three, when he took his first real job. He went to work as an editor for two prominent publishing houses—first Scholastic, then the company that owned *Parade* and Condé Nast.

For the next twenty years, he lived his work. At thirty-nine, on the brink of the Midlife Passage, he was predictably overwhelmed by a hurry-up sense. "Absolutely—hurry up and have a family." He and his career-directed partner moved in together and immediately set about making children. It took a while to produce twins and a few years later they had a son. His wife was intent on building her own literary agency. And Lee drove himself to reach the top editorial post in magazine journalism, working nights and weekends. Named editor in chief of *Parade* at the age of forty-seven, he had all the accoutrements of public success: a stable of writers, standing reservations at top restaurants, and a meaningful platform to influence public opinion with the largest audience of readers in the English-speaking world.

After fifty, the passages of our lives are largely unpredictable. They are often precipitated by a life accident—a blowout in our infrastructure, an unexpected divorce, the sudden death of a parent or a contemporary, or the shock of a full stop in career acceleration. That was the brutal wake-up call for Lee Kravitz. He was stopped in the hallway of *Parade* and told, "You are no longer the editor of this magazine." He was fifty-four. Being fired after fifty is a five-alarm wake-up call for anyone, but this was late 2007 and the U.S. economy was on the brink of an abyss. Kravitz had no plan B.

In the first weeks of being homebound, Kravitz realized he was not only a stranger to his wife and three children, he was not connected to himself. And when you are not connected to yourself, you cannot really feel the joy and compassion in being connected to other people. Our increasingly success- and profit-oriented culture does not favor executives who lead well-balanced lives. Kravitz was candid with me, as he is throughout this book. "When you're in a high-powered career, you give lip service to the idea of taking time off when your kids are born and date nights with your wife," said the former workaholic. "It just doesn't happen. You push yourself and the people you manage. My identity was my work. My role in the world was my work. I lost sight of who I really was."

This is a passage that can lead to a cosmic shift for some men. It begins with nurturing themselves. After half a century of racing forward through a series of passages assumed to lead to the peak of happiness and security, Kravitz sensed he had left some of the best of himself behind. Why? No time. Friendships that once throbbed with meaning had been allowed to lapse. Why? No time. Ties to his "messed-up family" of origin had frayed. Why? No effort to repair them. It began to dawn on him that he could only go forward by going back. Attending to "unfinished business" could be a way of rediscovering himself.

He knew he had taken the right direction when, "all of a sudden, at fifty-four, I felt compassion for my father. It was an opening up of my heart," he told me. "That was a huge life change, when you can look at someone so crucial to your view of yourself, and realize, 'I love him, I can't make him someone he isn't, I can just listen to him.'" For many men over fifty who I've interviewed, going back to recover lapsed parts of themselves turns out to be just what they need to shift from a laser focus on outer success to a discovery of the foreign realm of their inner lives. Many feel an urge to express their creative side. There is a hunger to be more connected to other people and to their community. They may move from a primary emphasis on competing to a broader sense of compassion.

There is an evolutionary basis for this observation. Charles Darwin, in his first book about humans, *The Descent of Man*, noted that the strongest instincts in early man were sympathy and compassion. Among our hominid predecessors, he argued, it was the communities of sympathetic individuals who were more successful in raising healthy offspring to the age when they too could reproduce. That was the surest route to getting their genes to the next generation. It was a radical claim, widely discounted by later social psychologists who argued that man is primarily motivated by raw self-interest to be selfish, greedy, and competitive. Recent scientific studies of emotion, however, by social psychologists like Dacher Keltner and the psychology lab at the University of California,

Berkeley, are finding evidence that humans are hardwired for compassion and caring. These are biologically based emotions rooted deep in the mammalian brain. That makes it entirely plausible that natural selection has favored humans who adapted to the need to care for the vulnerable.

Readers will find that this shift of emphasis from competing to connecting runs all through Kravitz's moving memoir of healing and rediscovery. Going back over the human business we leave unfinished because it is painful or inconvenient takes time and courage. But the joy in recovering lost pieces of one's heart is palpable on many pages of this book. The life lesson Lee Kravitz has to pass on to all of us is this: "It's finding compassion for oneself that allows you to have compassion for others. And that can open the way to vibrant human connectedness."

Gail Sheehy
February 2011

Compiling the List

Ten Things That Truly Matter

FOR OVER A year, things had been going downhill at work. A growing rift had opened up between me and my boss. It was hard to pinpoint what had gone wrong, but the affection and trust we once shared had steadily diminished. Unless things changed, either he would fire me or I would need to quit.

It was a tough admission to make, because I loved my job and I had assumed that I would be working there the rest of my life.

As the months wore on, my boss shunned me and I felt increasingly marginalized. I made attempts to change our dynamic, but nothing seemed to work. I kept my game face on around my colleagues and got done what needed to be done. At home, however, I sulked and felt sorry for myself and was irritable around the kids. On the last Sunday in September, Elizabeth and I were looking out across the lake, watching a flock of Canada geese lift from the water and set their sights south.

"I wouldn't mind joining them," I said.

"You'd take your computer along and spend the whole flight working," she said.

"I wouldn't," I said. "I'm dreading going to work tomorrow."

"I know," she said, putting her hand over mine. "Maybe it's time to leave."

I felt ready to move on, something I had never seen myself doing before.

* * *

THE NEXT MORNING, when I arrived at the office, an executive of the company told me that I no longer had a job. Because the conversation lasted less than a minute and took place in a hallway, I thought he was joking. But it wasn't a joke; I had been fired.

I called Elizabeth. In the few minutes it took for her to call me back, I went through a gamut of emotions: I was numb, then angry. I felt manipulated and betrayed. I had been tried, sentenced, and banished from the kingdom without a trial. Part of me expected my boss's boss to overturn the decision—a fantasy, of course. But mostly I felt humiliated. My father had lost his job when I was a teenager and nothing good ever came of it. No one in our family got any closer, wiser, or more giving as a result of his being unemployed. Instead, the loss of his job ushered in years of worry and fear. Now I was the one who had failed my family. How could I explain to my three young children that their father who worked all the time didn't work anymore? How could I protect them from everything that had confused and scared me when my own dad lost his job?

By the time Elizabeth reached me, I was too exhausted to talk. "I know how bad you're feeling," she said. "But in a few days you'll realize that this is the best thing that could have happened to you." I hoped she was right.

AT FIRST I tried to make up for lost time. I took the kids to school, saw all of their ball games, and helped them with their homework. I made plans to work out, lose weight, and lower my blood pressure. It was fun to go to museums with Elizabeth again; we hadn't done that in years.

Within weeks, though, I began feeling nervous and self-conscious about not working. Instead of seeing friends again, I stopped taking their phone calls. Instead of playing with the kids, I took naps. Instead of going on dates with Elizabeth, I stayed home to watch episodes of *Law & Order* I had already seen.

I'd stay in bed until ten or eleven in the morning, thinking about the moment I was fired and the people who had been responsible for firing me. I'd make a pot of coffee and drink cup after cup, until I was so wired that I couldn't stay focused on reading the paper or watching the news. Not having work preoccupied me as much as work had, and I thought about it constantly: when I took out the garbage, waved to a neighbor, or walked Pip, our dog. Because I had never anticipated being in this position, I had given no thought to what I might do next in my life. The realization unnerved me, to the point that I avoided the possibility of any conversation that might lead to another person asking me about my plans.

ELIZABETH SUGGESTED THAT I spend a few days at Kripalu, a yoga retreat in the Berkshires. She said that I might be able to relax there and gather my thoughts. When I shrugged her off, she handed me the phone.

On a rainy afternoon in late October, I set off from our home in Upstate New York and drove north on the Taconic and east on Interstate 90 into western Massachusetts. Most of the leaves had changed color and fallen by then, and I strained through the rain and my windshield wipers to make out Exit 2, which would take me to Routes 7 and 20 and the winding road to the town of Lenox. Somehow I got there and a little beyond—to the huge building that had once housed a Roman Catholic monastery.

Most of the people wandering through Kripalu's lobby were in their early to midfifties and looked a lot like I suppose I did—stressed out and clueless. I registered at the desk and dropped my duffel bag off at the room I was sharing with three other middle-aged men.

After a dinner of lentil soup, kale, and sweet potatoes, I had a choice of attending a movement class or a lecture on the Bhagavad Gita. Along with a dozen or so other people, I decided to spend my evening moving free-form to the rhythms of two drummers from the Caribbean.

At first I felt silly, flailing my arms back and forth like the Hindu goddess Durga. I felt even sillier when a man with a graying pony-tail pulled me into a circle of other mainly middle-aged men and women. But gradually I started to relax and enjoy myself, moving faster and faster over the hardwood floor in my bare feet. When our circle broke in two, we slithered around the room like a giant undu-lating snake. As the drumming reached its climax, we shed each other one by one and collapsed into a pile of sweat-soaked gigglers.

Proud of the progress I was making toward becoming the chilled-out father my kids wanted me to be, I retired to my dorm room and fell fast asleep.

The next morning I went to a six A.M. yoga class and had a break-fast of rolled oats, pumpkin seeds, and green tea. When I returned to the dorm room to shower, there was a note on my bed summon-ing me to the front office. An attractive young woman confided to me that two of my dorm mates had complained about my snoring, Kripalu's cardinal sin. She directed me to the snorers-only floor, Kripalu's Siberia.

The rejection by my dorm mates felt as piercing and punitive as losing my job. Less than a month earlier, I had been an important man, with an office and a secretary. Now I was just another snorer.

I WASN'T YOUR typical garden-variety, nine-to-five, you-can-invite-him-over-for-a-drink snorer. I was a workaholic snorer. And it had taken a huge toll on my family.

For years Elizabeth had been telling me, "You're never there for me." And I wasn't. Even when I was home, I was thinking about work. Did I appreciate the fact that Elizabeth did 80 percent of the child rearing and even more of the chores? Of course not. I had too much work to do. Did I make even the smallest effort to lessen her load? Sometimes, but mainly because I wanted to get ahead of the curve so she would let me work in peace.

The worst part of being so focused on my work was the relationship it kept me from having with my children. Benjamin said he was afraid to approach me, and his twin sister, Caroline, told the babysitter, "Daddy never smiles." They were almost eleven and beginning to pull away. Noah, who was nearing eight, still liked to crawl into bed with Elizabeth and me and cuddle. But to enjoy his affection, I needed to be in our bed and not in my study, working on my computer.

Easier said than done.

Being a workaholic was in my genes. My father was a workaholic, and so were my grandfather and great-grandfather, a Lithuanian peasant who got up at three A.M. to plow his fields.

In a world that valued hard work, no one worked harder than a Kravitz. Of course most of the Kravitz men died of heart attacks in their early sixties, and most of them had only a handful of friends, but you could never accuse a Kravitz of slacking off: We lived to work and worked until it killed us.

And society fed our disease. In my twenty years in corporate America, I was seldom told to work less, and when I was, the boss saying it didn't mean it, unless he was under strict orders from his own boss to cut overtime. You did not get promoted for being a good husband, father, or friend, or for volunteering for the local school board, or for taking time off, even when you had earned it. You got ahead by being perceived as an employee who worked day and night and put your job first. You didn't get a raise by attending your child's teacher conferences or by leaving your BlackBerry off. You got it by beating your boss to the office each morning and working through lunch. By working weekends and holidays and on vacations. And by always being in touch.

All of these thoughts came to me during my week at Kripalu. I didn't reach nirvana there, but I did gain perspective on what my dedication to work had cost me, and it made me less eager to find another job. Not that I could have found one: I was a fifty-four-year-old magazine editor in an industry that was hemorrhaging jobs and going through a period of fundamental change. With Elizabeth's income and my severance pay, we could get by for maybe a year. I could spend that year learning new skills with which to reenter the job market. Or I could spend it making myself a happier and more appreciative person, with richer friendships and a far better sense of who I was and what genuinely mattered to me. That's what I really wanted to do, but how and where would I begin?

THE ANSWER CAME by accident in the form of ten cardboard boxes that had been sent to our country house from my old workplace. The boxes had spent the last thirteen years in a closet there, and they contained everything I had saved from the previous four decades of my life.

Why had I kept the boxes at work? Because there was no room for them in our tiny Manhattan apartment. Why hadn't I moved them to our country house before? Because I was always working and didn't have time to think about them or the distracting memories they might contain.

But now I did. I gave myself a week in the country to sort through the boxes and organize the accumulated stuff of my life. Elizabeth and the kids were in the city, so I had the run of the house and room to spread things out. It would be one of those big, messy projects that I both loved and hated to do. I would need to make piles of what to keep in the country, what to keep in the city, and what to throw away. I would need to make decisions I dreaded and create a lot more chaos before I saw even a semblance of order.

It would be a considerable undertaking but not without its own pleasures. So I poured myself a glass of wine and raised it in a toast to the project ahead. Because I wanted anything I did to help me become a better father to my kids, I queued up one of my son Noah's favorite songs, the Beatles' "Eight Days a Week." Then I went to work.

After opening the first few boxes, I realized how impatient I must have been when I packed them: Files of notes and essays from college shared the same box as a giant map of Central America and my bronzed baby shoes. My letter jacket from high school covered memorabilia I had collected at the 1992 Republican and Democratic Conventions.

One box contained my report cards since kindergarten, carefully stapled by my mother into two piles, the good and the bad. There was a list of friends and later girlfriends at ages seven, eleven, nineteen, and twenty-six, and eulogies I had written for family pets, my maternal grandmother, and a friend who died of cancer.

In another box there were more than a thousand letters from my father, one per week since college, featuring his distinctive use of brackets, quotation marks, and red type for emphasis. My roommates and I had spent hours trying to decode my father's letters for secret messages. We never found any. But we did find plenty of Knute Rockne–type advice and coaching. My father's letters baffled but also compelled me, so I kept them all. There was a collection of my old baseball caps in the box, along with an Indonesian shadow puppet I had purchased in Bali.

The boxes were full of strange and wonderful juxtapositions, but what struck me most was how the different objects reflected parts of myself I had suppressed or forgotten. The machete I used when I harvested bananas on a kibbutz in Israel reminded me of the thirst I once had for adventure. A barely decipherable dream journal brought back a year when I was so poor and scared for my future that I couldn't sleep at night but got by with a little help from my friends.

There was a box containing the notebooks and memorabilia that my grandfather gave me two weeks before he died. He spent the last two decades of his life creating businesses that gave jobs and dignity to the survivors of the Holocaust. He was my biggest hero at a time when I still believed in them.

That same box contained a copy of my high school yearbook. Flipping through it, I experienced dozens of where-is-he-now, why-didn't-I-keep-up-with-him feelings of curiosity and regret. I noticed, for example, that the photo of my childhood bully was directly across from mine, reinforcing my sense that he had been born to torment me. There was also a photo of my favorite teacher, a young Episcopal priest who inspired me to think and write and believe in my obligation to do good in the world. I had fallen out of touch with him, just as I had with my soul mate in high school, a boy who had opened my eyes to the possibility of experiencing God and who later became a monk.

Life goes fast. Click. You are fifteen. Click, click. You are fifty-five. Click, click. You are gone. And so are the people who loved and nurtured you.

In one box there was a doctor's report confirming that my mother's mother, my beloved Nana Bertie, could no longer live on her own. When I was six, she taught me how to play Fish. When I was eight, she accused me of cheating. When I was twelve, fifteen, seventeen, and twenty-one, she came to my graduations and told everyone how proud she was of me, even though I cheated at Fish.

I found a photo of one of the few times in twenty-five years that my brothers and I gathered in the same place at the same time with our wives and children. One of those times was at my wedding, when Elizabeth was six months pregnant with our twins. Why didn't we get together more often? Busy working, the family disease.

How quickly it all goes: There were photos of me with and without a beard and in various stages of baldness over thirty years, a jar that contained the ashes of our poodle Buster, a letter from a friend in London who had been waiting for me to travel to Paris with him to visit the grave of Jim Morrison of the Doors, photos of Joyce and me at my high school prom. She was my first love and we were still friends fifteen years later when she was killed in an automobile accident as she was driving home from her wedding shower. She was buried two days later, on the same afternoon that she was supposed to get married. Joyce and I had always said that we'd be friends until we were eighty. That dreary September day she died was one of the saddest of my life.

I poured myself a second glass of wine and looked quickly through another box. Tucked into a folder of postage stamps from around the world, I found a torn copy of the prayer I said each night until I was ten years old. I still knew the words by heart:

> *Before in sleep I close my eyes;*
> *To thee, O God, my thoughts arise;*
> *I thank thee for thy blessings all*
> *That come to us, thy children small.*
> *O keep me safe throughout the night*
> *So I shall see the morning light.*

Nearly fifty years had passed since I had first said that prayer, yet in so many ways I still felt like the child who had said it.

I DID NOT fall asleep easily that blustery night. Encountering the past this way—all at once and out of chronology and context—disrupted my everyday sense of things and even of myself. When I closed my eyes, I found myself reexperiencing a footrace I'd almost won, my bar mitzvah speech, and the summer of 1969, when I lost my virginity and helped pitch my sandlot team to the state championship.

That game had taken place on a hot summer day before a crowd that included major league scouts, small-time gamblers, and suntanned teenage girls. As I lay awake, I thought about Andre, our right fielder, who was a superb athlete and an even better human being. Although I hadn't seen him since that long-ago summer, I had recently seen a photo of his daughter in the *New York Times*. She had been ambushed and killed on a peace mission to Iraq. Putting myself in Andre's place, I had cried and cried. Somehow I still hadn't written my old teammate to tell him how sorry I was for his loss.

Other realizations of what I should have done but didn't came to mind and kept me from finding sleep.

Earlier that evening, I had listened to an interview with my nana Shirley in the late 1970s. Hearing my grandmother tell her old stories in her familiar Yiddish made me smile and miss her terribly. But now I remembered that I had skipped her funeral because I had so much work to do the week she died.

The moonlight streamed through the curtains and lit up my bedroom. I remembered a trip I had once made to a refugee camp in northern Kenya. The camp was hot and dusty and housed more than thirty-two thousand children who had been uprooted from their homes by the tribal wars in neighboring Somali. Most of those children would never see their parents again, and yet they clung to the idea of a better life. I met one boy who wanted me to tell him everything I could about America because he dreamed of going there someday. He showed me a musty textbook he'd been reading to improve his English. It was from the days when Kenya was still a colony of the British Empire. I told him that I would fill the camp's library with new books, ones he would like.

"That's what everyone says," he said, shrugging his shoulders as if to indicate that I probably wouldn't.

I hadn't, and I hadn't let it trouble me for years.

I must have nodded off for a while because when I opened my eyes the shadows had shifted in the room. But again my thoughts returned to the boxes. Their contents attested to the rich human connections I had forged earlier in my life. But they also contained evidence of my unfinished business: tasks like paying a condolence call to Andre that I had either put off or failed to follow through on. For a variety of reasons—my self-involvement, my hurry to get ahead, a sense that I would get to them later—I had neglected matters of great consequence. In the process, I had hurt the people closest to me and fed the fear and compulsion that had kept me chained to my job.

There were signs in these boxes that there had been a better me: a more curious, adventurous, and compassionate individual who had taken risks to do the right thing. Too often, though, my fears had taken over, creating the unfinished business that kept holding me back.

If I had committed a bank robbery or traffic violation, I would have gone to jail, paid a fine, or been sentenced to community service. Yet no one could prosecute me for missing my grandmother's funeral or failing to keep a promise to a child—no one except me.

There are acts and nonacts that prosecute you from within. They trouble your soul and cast aspersion on your character. They tell you that you are callous, small-minded, less than you want to be. Isn't it strange how small these things can seem on paper, yet how large they loom in your head? Before I finally fell asleep, I concluded that I would condemn myself to piling up even more unfinished business unless I attended to some of it now.

By the time I woke up the next morning, I was ready to make a plan. Instead of rushing out to find a job, I would devote an entire year to tying up my loose emotional ends.

OVER THE NEXT few days, I spent a good deal of time meditating on how I wanted to proceed. One of the biggest urges I felt was to make amends. It was the most human of impulses and one that most religions put at the center of their promises of forgiveness and heaven.

When a person died in ancient Egypt, his heart would be weighed to determine if his soul would make it into the afterlife. If a person's heart weighed less than a feather and was judged pure, the soul got in. If the heart, burdened by sin, weighed more than a feather, the soul lost its spot.

Buddhism says that we accumulate good karma from our right actions and bad karma from our wrong ones, as does Hinduism. Picture walking around with a big bag of bad karma over your shoulder; it weighs you down and holds you back. How do you lessen the load so that you can move ahead in this life and the next? Through right actions, Buddhist lamas say.

In confessing their sins to a priest, Catholics acknowledge their flawed nature before God and express their willingness to make up for it.

On Yom Kippur, the Jewish Day of Atonement, we fast and pray. I used to love Yom Kippur when I was a kid. At temple I would stand next to my father, lightly beating my chest as we recited the sins we had committed.

We would elbow each other when we thought a sin was particularly applicable. "For the sin which we have committed before Thee by spurning parents and teachers." (I got elbowed.) "For the sin we have committed before Thee by hardening our hearts." (I elbowed him.) "For the sin we have committed before Thee by denying and lying." (I got elbowed.) "For the sin we have committed before Thee by stretching the neck in pride." (I got elbowed, then him.) It would go on and on for another dozen sins until we would say, in unison, "For all these, O God of forgiveness, forgive us, pardon us, grant us atonement."

On Yom Kippur, God forgave us for all the vows we wouldn't fulfill in the coming year. But he only gave us absolution for the vows that involved him. It was much harder to atone for the sins we committed against other people. We had to ask the person to forgive us. If he chose not to, the wrong would persist. So you had to be precise—and persuasive—in your amends.

In Judaism, as in the other religious traditions, sincerity is what

counts most. You must cease to commit a sin, really regret it, and resolve not to do it again. I have never participated in a twelve-step
program, but I do know that making amends is an important part of
the recovery process. In Alcoholics Anonymous, for example, you are
instructed to make a list of everyone you have harmed and express a
sincere willingness to repair the hurt. It is not enough to just apolo-
gize. You must endeavor to make *direct* amends, and put your money
(or whatever is appropriate recompense) where your mouth is.

Addicts are more likely than other people to lie, steal, cheat, and
commit adultery. Imagine how much bad karma an addict carries
around in his bag. Imagine how much hard work and willpower it
takes for him to lessen his load.

Did I have that much courage and discipline? That was what
I wondered as I compiled my list of unfinished business.

I SHOULD HAVE made that condolence call to Andre and gone to
my grandmother's funeral and kept my promise to the boy in Kenya
and done a thousand other things that I failed to do. As I compiled
my list, I knew why each of these items was important to me. But it
took months for me to understand the underlying patterns that had
made each of them so difficult for me to address. It isn't the easy
tasks that become our unfinished business; it's the hard ones, the
ones we are most afraid to face.

If I had gone to my grandmother's funeral, I would have had to
face the reality of my messed-up family. Writing the condolence
card to Andre brought fears of my own daughter's death. The boy
in the refugee camp represented the suffering of all the world's children to me, and my limited ability to help.

The items on my list of unfinished business were linked to my
deepest feelings of helplessness, disappointment, and fear. It's ironic:
We consign our most essential business to the bottom of our to-do
list because we lack the time and energy to do the things that matter

most in our lives well. It makes sense: The most important things take the most time and energy and we have only so much time and energy in a day. You let things slide. But I would also discover the corollary to this in the coming months: that, if one can attend to these things, great rewards will follow.

MY YEAR OF taking care of my unfinished business would take the form of ten separate journeys. Three of those journeys involved my family, including my parents and grandparents, my uncles and aunts, and the near and distant relatives who shared in my family's good times and savaged each other when things went bad. Family, the core of who we are, was the source of my most intimate and anxiety-producing unfinished business.

My other seven journeys focused on four old friends, a former rival, my first mentor, and a boy I barely knew. In reaching out to them, I sought to either close a circle or right a wrong.

Some type of fear played a role in creating all of the unfinished business I needed to complete. Simply taking the time to do the right thing often seemed impossible. On top of this anxiety, I was also afraid of doing something stupid or insensitive. Or I was afraid of letting someone down. To deal with these fears, even to identify them, took time—something I seldom had or gave to myself. But, as I would learn, when I did take the time and reached out in the right spirit and with compassion and persevered, something remarkable would happen. I wouldn't only right a wrong, I would reconnect with parts of myself that I had forgotten. And having jumped in, I would find myself in a place of rich, exuberant humanity.

I didn't know any of that in the beginning, or even if my project was doable. All I really knew at the time was that I needed to find my aunt Fern. When I was a child, Fern babysat me. When I was older, she confided in me and we shared our dreams. Fern was the only person in my family who always seemed to be there for me.

And then fifteen years ago, she was institutionalized after a fight with my grandmother. They had been living together in my grandmother's apartment, and in their frustration—Fern was schizophrenic, my grandmother had Alzheimer's—they screamed and tore at each other until the authorities took Fern away.

Whenever I asked, no one in my family would claim to know where Fern was—not even my father, who was her brother. And no one seemed to care. I found their lack of concern—and my own over the years—unconscionable. That's why I needed to find Fern— to show both her and myself that I cared.

CHAPTER ONE

Searching for Sorrow's Daughter

Finding a Long-Lost Relative

AS I WAS combing through the artifacts of my past, I had come across a card that my aunt Fern sent to me for my thirty-third birthday.

The card featured a drawing of a kimono-clad woman painting a delicate Japanese landscape. Inside, there was a poem by Robert Browning Hamilton, which Fern had printed out in small, carefully wrought letters:

I walked a mile with Pleasure
She chatted all the way;
But left me none the wiser
For all she had to say.

I walked a mile with Sorrow
And ne'er a word said she.
But, oh! The things I learned from her
When Sorrow walked with me.

"I love you so much, Ricky," Fern added, using my family nickname. Then she wrote, "P.S., It's a long story—someday we'll write it together."

When I first got that card, more than twenty years ago, I remember feeling that someday I would help Fern share the lessons she had learned during her walk with Sorrow. "It's a long story—someday we'll write it together." That was my pact with Fern, and hers with me.

But the fact was, I hadn't seen or heard from my aunt in nearly fifteen years. What's more, no one in my family seemed to know or care where Fern was.

MY AUNT FERN suffered from schizophrenia and had been living in and out of mental institutions since she was thirteen years old. As a child she had trained to become a concert pianist. But when her tantrums got worse and her moods became erratic, her doctors medicated her and sent a current of electricity into her brain. When she was younger, Fern was petite and pretty, a suburban Jewish princess. But her medication made her obese. By the time she was thirty, my four-foot-ten-inch aunt weighed over two hundred pounds. Fern married the captain of the high school football team. The day they divorced, she slit her wrists, the first of several suicide attempts that landed her in the psych ward. After her last hospitalization, in 1994, Fern's doctors discouraged family members from seeing her. They were afraid that we would trigger memories in Fern and drive her deeper into despair.

That birthday card reminded me of how much Fern had loved me and also meant to me. Of all my relatives, she was the one who encouraged me to follow my heart. Fern may have seen an assassin lurking behind every bush, but she urged me and the rest of her nieces and nephews to love the world and everything in it, including ourselves. Why did I want to see her? There were many reasons, from wanting to make amends to sharing stories about my childhood to showing Fern that someone cares. But I also was drawn to Fern by the prospect of getting a little unconditional love at a time when I probably needed it.

It was as though I had buried my feelings for Fern and forgotten about them. Then one day I stumbled on them in the form of that beautiful old card and they came flooding back. But where was she?

The last time I saw her, Fern was fifty-two. She would be sixty-six now. If anyone knew where she was, it would be Trina, her first cousin. According to my father, it was Trina who had conveyed the message from Fern's doctors that we weren't allowed to see her.

My last encounter with Trina had not been a happy one. After I graduated from journalism school, I told her that I was thinking about writing an article about a cousin of hers known to have close ties with the mafia. Trina bristled at the idea. "Ricky," she said, "let Jackie be Jackie." Then she walked away.

That was twenty-five years ago.

As I booked my tickets for Cleveland, I must confess that the prospect of asking Trina where Fern was unnerved me.

IN THE HOME movie that runs through my mind, it is Fern on piano who provides the background music for my family's happiest occasions. We are standing around my grandmother's baby grand as Fern plays and the rest of us sing the music of the era: "Camelot, Camelot" . . . "The hills are alive with the sound of music" . . . "Moon River, wider than a mile" . . . "Shall we dance, shall we dance, shall we dance."

All of us are singing: my mother, my brothers, even my father; my grandmother, her three sisters, my cousins. Some of us sing in tune, most of us do not, and the rest of us are mouthing the lyrics pretending to be Julie Andrews, Ethel Merman, or Robert Goulet. Grandpa Benny is the only one not singing. He's sitting in his favorite chair, tapping his pipe and feet in time to the music. He is smiling for a change. We all are.

ON THE FLIGHT from New York to Cleveland, I thought about those Friday night dinners at my grandmother's house, and about the night we sat shiva for my grandfather. It was on October 20, 1972. I had just begun my sophomore year in college when my

father called with the news of Grandpa's death. I took the first
plane back to Cleveland. As my father drove me to the funeral home,
he said, "I'll never be the man my father was." It was the only time
I ever saw him cry.

That night, a union boss who'd flown up from Cincinnati told
stories that offended the women and made the men laugh so hard
they choked. At one point, Fern grabbed my arm and said, "Ricky,
did you see him?" She pointed in the direction of the marble foyer.
"Did you see him, Ricky?" She had just seen my grandfather's ghost
walking through the foyer. A few hours later she tried to kill herself.

WHILE MOST OF my relatives avoided Fern, I was her confidante.
Because I read philosophy and wrote poetry, because I traveled to
far-off places and had stories to tell, Fern considered me the member of the family who was sensitive enough to understand her. In a
family that didn't value empathy—my father equated it with weak-
ness, my mother said it would get me nowhere fast—Fern considered it a strength.

After I moved to New York in the early 1980s, I made a point of
seeing Fern and her husband whenever I visited Cleveland. Fern's
second husband, Jerry, was a fast-talking gambler who dressed like
a member of the Rat Pack. They never had children, but they did
get a terror of a terrier named Buffy who shredded everything in
sight. They lived with Nana Shirley in an apartment that was all
white except for my grandmother's black baby grand. As the years
wore on, Fern and Jerry's incessant smoking took a toll on the
apartment, turning the walls first yellow, then a sickly beige.

Our routine was always the same. I would arrive at the apartment at five P.M. and make small talk while Fern and Jerry smoked
in the living room. At five forty-five P.M., in time for the early bird
specials, I drove them to their favorite Chinese restaurant, at a

nearby mall. They always ordered won ton soup, egg rolls, spicy spare ribs, and chicken chow mein. While Nana and Jerry picked at the appetizers, Fern pulled me aside to tell me her secrets: how men had always liked her, how some had abused her, how she was scared to death that her beloved Gerald would get sick and die.

When Jerry had his first heart attack, Fern took care of him: "My job isn't an easy one," she wrote to me. "I must bathe him, change his surgical dressings, help him dress, walk and make sure he gets enough rest. I hope you are proud of me," she added. "Your love, devotion and respect mean so much to me and always did." No one else in my life wrote sentences like that to me. No one else was so open and loving and vulnerable.

As Jerry's condition worsened, so did Fern's handwriting and state of mind. The week before he died, Fern sent me the following note, in a spidery, shaky hand: "Dear idealistic nephew of mine, try to enjoy your life and experiences and try to tolerate the people you concern yourself with."

She was urging me to maintain my idealism in the face of the heartbreak and tragedy that would inevitably challenge me, as they had challenged her.

WHEN I LAST saw Fern and my grandmother together, it was with Elizabeth, the woman I intended to marry. I wanted Elizabeth to meet two of the most important women in my life, and for Fern and my grandmother to see that after all those years of dating women of other faiths, I would be marrying a Jew. Nana Shirley was frail with Alzheimer's and Fern was still numb from grief, but I do think, on some level, they understood that Elizabeth was the woman who would become my wife and raise my children in a Jewish household.

During the year before the incident that separated my grandmother and Fern, I didn't get a chance to visit Cleveland. I was busy, as always, at work. But that was also the year that Elizabeth and I started living together in an apartment we had rented in Brooklyn. It was a new life, and our first big step toward getting married. Then, one evening Elizabeth's mother called us from Detroit in tears. Elizabeth's brother had just been killed in a car accident, after being hit by a drunken teen. Elizabeth and her family went into a deep depression. It was two years before we could even think of getting married.

So perhaps, when Fern and my grandmother got into their fight and were separated from each other, I was preoccupied by the tragedy in Elizabeth's family or numb to more bad news. And when my grandmother died, I didn't attend her funeral because I couldn't imagine dealing with my bickering relatives. Maybe work was only an excuse. Maybe I didn't stay involved in Fern's life because I was tired of all the sadness and just wanted to get married and create my own life with Elizabeth. I abandoned Fern for many reasons. Fifteen years later, I was ready to make amends.

TRINA AND I decided to meet at the house of a mutual friend.

"I can't believe it's been fifty years since I used to babysit you, Ricky. I can't get used to Lee. Can I call you Ricky, Ricky?"

"Of course," I said. "Consider yourself a charter member of the very exclusive club of people who call me by a name I haven't used since I was nine years old."

Trina laughed. Although her face had toughened with age, she was a handsome woman, with dark brown hair and light green eyes, and she could name-drop with the best of them, particularly when it came to the ties between her cousin Jackie's union and the Cleveland mob.

Trina had gambled with Jackie's mother, lived at Jackie's house, and run an antiques store with his third wife, a looker named Carmen.

"Whatever happened to her?" I asked.

Trina then told me the best story I'd heard in ages, about how she and Carmen played a role in Jackie's downfall. The story happened around the time the mob found out that Jackie informed on them to the FBI.

"If the mob knew that, why didn't they kill him?" I asked.

"Because Jackie was dying from brain cancer," Trina said. "And they wanted him to suffer the most painful death possible."

"And how about Fern?" I slipped in. "Do you have any idea where she is?"

Trina didn't bother to dodge the question. "She's at a special-care facility in Aurora, about a half hour away. My social worker friend Eva helped me find the place."

"Why did you do it?" I asked.

"Do what?"

"Go to all that trouble to help Fern," I said.

"Because your grandmother was like a second mother to me and Fern and I were like sisters. And for whatever reason—I don't judge—your father and his brother did not want to get involved."

It had taken me fifteen years to start even thinking about Fern. So who was I to judge my father or my uncle for not getting involved? Trina had been the only person in the family to reach out to Fern. Thank God, I thought, for Trina.

EN ROUTE TO Aurora Manor I missed two exits and drove twenty miles west before I realized that I should have been going east. By the time I pulled into the parking lot it was eleven A.M. and I would need to leave by twelve thirty P.M. to make my plane to New York.

"Can I help you?" the receptionist said.

I didn't really know where to begin. "My aunt is here. I haven't seen her in almost fifteen years. I don't want to upset her. Is there anyone I can talk with, to see how she's doing, to see if I can see her?"

"Who are you here to visit?" the woman said.

"Fern Litt."

"I'll buzz her social worker. Have a seat."

When I first walked into the special-care facility, I expected to enter a world of cold, heartless institutional gray, as in the film *One Flew Over the Cuckoo's Nest.* But as I waited in the lobby, I noticed how inviting the place was, with fresh flowers, green and orange sofas, and painted landscapes on the wall.

An attractive woman with glasses and a professional yet warm demeanor walked up to me.

"Hi. I'm Allison," she said. "I'm Fern's social worker. I understand that you'd like to see her."

"If it wouldn't upset her," I said.

"It shouldn't," she said. "But Fern doesn't get many visitors. You're the first relative of hers I've ever met."

"Has Fern had any visitors at all?" I asked.

"Only one," she said. "A young woman named Tania. She was the daughter of one of the residents here and she visited Fern a couple of times after her mother died."

Fern had had only one visitor in fourteen years.

I followed Allison into the dining room, where the residents were eating lunch. Most of the residents had white hair and seemed much older than Fern would have been.

"So how is she?" I asked.

"Confused," Allison said. "But she can ask for something when she needs it—for example, a cigarette or help dressing—and the nurses here love Fern because she's such a kind and warm person and she's led such an interesting life."

I looked around the room. No one even remotely resembled my aunt. "Does she remember anything?" I asked Allison.

"Some things. She'll talk about her travels. And about playing the piano when she was young. We're always trying to get her to play."

"Does she?"

"No. But I bet she'd like to."

"What else does she do?

"Smoke. She really loves to smoke."

As Allison and I talked, a nurse with blazing red hair steered a wheelchair through the tables of white-haired seniors. I could barely make its occupant out. But then the wheelchair came toward me. The first thing I noticed was her hair—or rather the lack of it, since there were only a few black strands covering her head. Her face was pancake round and her eyes darted up and down behind her thick eyeglasses like ping-pong balls. I then noticed that her hands were shaking wildly. They poked through her hospital gown, along with her plump legs, white ankle socks, and slippers. The closer the wheelchair got to us, the more her hands shook, like a toddler who couldn't wait to open a Christmas gift. And then Fern said, "Lee Richard Kravitz, my brilliant nephew. I can't believe it, everyone. Lee Richard Kravitz is here to see me."

I was too stunned to talk.

Fern gestured for me to hug her and we held each other tightly. "I thought I'd never see you again," she kept saying.

I felt the same way. I was afraid I'd never see her again. And if I did, that she wouldn't recognize me. Now we were holding each other as long and as tightly as I'd held anyone in years. There was nothing awkward or self-conscious about this embrace; it was primal, nourishing. I felt as if a huge weight had been lifted from my shoulders—the weight of not knowing if Fern was dead or alive, the weight of shutting her out of my mind, the weight of no longer being the person I had been to her.

I felt lighter just being in Fern's presence, and basked in her joy at seeing me.

Allison suggested that I wheel Fern into the courtyard for a smoke. Before doing so, an aide who supplied Fern with cigarettes placed a thick protective vest over her chest. "This will keep Fern safe," she told me.

"I burned myself," Fern said, with the look of puppy dog who knew that she had done something wrong. "I burned myself, Lee Richard. Right here," she said, pointing to a spot on her stomach. "And here."

There were four benches in the courtyard. I placed Fern's wheelchair by the bench closest to an ashtray.

"Permission to smoke?" she asked me.

"Of course," I said.

I lit a cigarette for her. She inhaled it deeply.

"How is my oldest brother, Harry?" she asked.

"He and my mother are living in Florida and they really like it there," I said.

"In Florida?" she said delightedly. "Harry's in Florida?"

"Yup. And his health is good, except for his hearing, of course. He's stone deaf."

"Stone deaf," she said, seeming genuinely sad for her older brother. "Permission to flick?"

"Permission granted," I said.

She flicked a long ash from her cigarette onto the ground, and then asked about my mother. "How's Phyllis? Is she happy?"

It was the most knowing question any one could have asked about my mom. When things were going well—when my father was working and she had enough money to buy clothes and go out with friends and get a piece of new furniture every few years—my mother could be the happiest woman on the planet. When things weren't going well—when my father was out of work and she had to take a job as a cashier at a department store and cater to women who wanted to be waited on, this minute, now—my mother could be miserable, self-pitying, and certain that she was a paycheck away from becoming a bag lady.

"She is in a lot of back pain from her years of cashiering, but she likes the weather and her friends," I said. "I'd say my mother is happy."

"Phyllis is happy," Fern said. "That's good."

I also told Fern the latest about my brothers and my cousins and their wives, husbands, and children. She remembered the names of everyone who had been born before she started living in Aurora Manor and was tickled to hear that she had a fourteen-year-old niece named Dakota. "Dakota. I have a niece named Dakota," she said again and again. At times, however, she would look over her shoulder quizzically. Finally, she said, "I don't know where I am, Lee Richard. I don't know where I am."

Fern had been at Aurora Manor for fourteen years and no one had told her where she was in terms that made sense to her.

I said that she was in a special-care facility in Aurora, Ohio. It was about half an hour away from the house where she grew up. She was even closer to the apartment she had shared with her mother and Jerry in Beachwood. Aurora Manor was just down the road from Geauga Lake Amusement Park, whose giant roller coaster had scared Fern when she was a kid. And she was only two miles away from Mount Olive Cemetery, where Jerry was buried.

"Thank you, Lee Richard," she said. "Thank you for telling me where I am."

I lit another cigarette for her. She told me how lonely she was, how she missed her mother, her brothers, and Jerry. She said that she had written six letters to three governors of Ohio, requesting that they allow her to leave. No one had written her back. "I'm a prisoner, Lee Richard, a prisoner," she said.

"And no one remembers my birthday, Lee Richard. Not Harry, not Pudgy, not anyone. November the fourth comes and goes and no one calls or sends me a card."

A plane flew by. Fern looked up, and then cowered as if she were afraid of getting bombed. I took out a photograph I had brought of my three children and Pip.

"These are your nephews Benjamin and Noah," I said. "We named Benjamin after Grandpa Benny. And here's your niece. Her name is Caroline. Isn't she pretty? And this is Pip, our dog. He is much better behaved than Buffy."

"Buffy," she laughed. "My bad dog Buffy."

Fern took the photograph and asked me what each of my children liked to do. I told her that Ben and Noah played baseball and the violin and that Caroline rode horses and played piano. When I said that she could keep the photo, she clutched it to her heart.

It was nearly time for me to catch my plane.

I walked a mile with Pleasure
She chatted all the way.
But I was none the wiser . . .

I couldn't believe my ears. Fern was reciting the poem that she had inscribed on the card she sent me on my thirty-third birthday. Did she remember writing "It's a long story—someday we'll write it together" on the card? Again, I was too stunned to ask.

"What a beautiful poem," I told her. "And you said it beautifully, with so much heart."

"Thank you," she said.

It was time for me to go. This had been one of the most extraordinary hours of my life, and I had gotten far more out of seeing Fern than simply righting my original wrong. I had helped Fern locate her place in the world in a way that made sense to her, but she had done the same for me. Fern brought out the part of me that acted selflessly and cared for those closest to me. It was a part of myself that I didn't see often enough.

"I need to go," I said, realizing that I would be back as soon as I could to see her.

"Don't leave, Lee Richard," she said.

"I have to," I said. "But I'll be back soon. I promise."

* * *

THE ONLY PEOPLE I told about Fern were Elizabeth, my parents, my brothers, and my uncle Pudge. I told my parents because I wanted them to know that Fern was alive and well taken care of and concerned about their health. I told my brothers because I thought it would be nice, if they had a chance, to visit her. And I told my uncle Pudge because I thought it was important for him to see his sister at least one more time before he died. Pudge had had a heart transplant in 1991 and I presumed, perhaps wrongly, that he was living on borrowed time.

The reaction from my father and uncle was more measured than I had expected. Both held fast to the idea that it would be harmful for them to see Fern.

My father wrote "I am amazed that you were able to find out where Fern is 'because Trina was very emphatic' about not providing me any information about her, indicating that it would 'not be in Fern's best interest, psychologically' for me to visit her according to the 'Professionals' who were assigned to her."

He commended me for finding and seeing Fern, but he also felt a need to put my trip into perspective. "I am certain that Fern 'felt your kindness in her Heart,' Lee. But, as I was warned by Fern's attending Psychiatrists over the years, you must not allow 'sympathy to blind you to reality.'"

I felt bad for my father. As Fern's oldest brother it had been his job to shuttle her back and forth from the psych ward and to handle whatever crisis came up in the middle of the night. Delegated by my grandparents to help her, he became the target of some of Fern's most violent tantrums. He prided himself on being the family's problem solver, but Fern had problems no older brother could ever solve.

In a sense, though, my father had missed the point of my visiting Fern. I didn't do it just for Fern, to show her that someone cared; I also did it for myself. And I wanted my father to be touched as I had been, to feel a weight lifting from *his* shoulders, to experience a softening and expansion of *his* heart.

Pudge's e-mail said, "The family failed Fern in one way or another. It took you, Lee, to make me realize my own failure. God bless you. As Sean Hannity would say, 'You are a great American.'"

A week later Pudge sent me another e-mail. "Now that I know where Fern is, I want to see her. Tell me what to do."

I told him what he needed to know: who to contact, how to get there, and what to expect. I also said, "After you see her, tell me everything that happened."

He did.

On a Sunday morning in late June, I met my uncle for coffee at a diner in Upstate New York. He was wearing a purple plaid shirt and pressed khaki pants. For a man who had weathered a heart transplant and many other infirmities over the years, he looked great.

"So?" I asked him.

"So, I saw her," he said.

"And?"

"It was amazing," he said. "No one could believe that Fern had a visitor. Allison called the nurses over and said, 'Guess who this is? It's Fern's brother.'"

Pudge's visit mirrored my own. When he hugged Fern, she wouldn't let go. He told her about his family. They reminisced about the past. She said how much she missed Jerry and Nana Shirley. When she asked about his wife, Pudge told her that Judy was in the lobby. When he brought Judy in, Fern said, "You don't need to be afraid of me," and the women hugged. Fern told Judy how she tried to keep the Sabbath but it was hard, she said, because she was the only Jew at Aurora Manor. When Pudge and Judy left, Fern said, "Shalom," the Hebrew word for hello, good-bye, and peace.

"It sounds like a wonderful visit," I said. "Are you happy you saw her?"

"Yeah," Pudge said. "It was one of the things I had left that I needed to do."

Pudge hadn't used the phrase, but it was clear that like me he had gone to Cleveland to complete a piece of his unfinished business.

When Pudge was fifty-seven, he had a heart attack. Because his arteries were so corroded, he was given another person's heart. After his heart transplant, Pudge started getting closer to the family in Cleveland again, but not to Fern and Harry. He had not seen Fern since before my grandmother died, and he had spoken only twice to my father in nearly thirty years—first at my grandmother's funeral, and then on a Chicago street corner at a surprise meeting engineered by one of my brothers and one of Pudge's kids. It did not go well. Upon seeing each other, Pudge said, "How are you feeling?"

"Pretty good," my father said.

"Well, you look good," replied Pudge. And they returned to their respective taxis.

The rift between Pudge and my father pained all of us. It was sad to see two brothers so deeply embittered by their ancient squabbles that they refused to acknowledge each other's existence or mention the other's name.

That Pudge had seen Fern and been moved by their encounter emboldened me to see if he wanted to try one more time with my father. I asked, "Now that you've seen Fern, would you like to see Harry again?"

Either he didn't hear me or chose not to respond, but I had planted a seed.

AFTER I RETURNED to New York, I tried to mail something to Fern at least twice a month. She had not received mail in more than fourteen years. It was fun to think of her showing the latest photo

of Pip and the kids to her friends and nurses and being proud that
her nephew in New York was thinking about her.

In August, I made my second visit to see my aunt. Ever since she
told me how sad she'd get when no one would acknowledge her
birthday, I had been thinking about throwing her a birthday party.
I wanted to get Allison's input before I started organizing it. "Would
Fern be able to handle all that attention?" I asked.

"She'd love it," Allison said.

Sally, Fern's nurse, also liked the idea. Whenever Fern needed
something—a new nightgown, for instance—she and her husband,
John, bought it for her. John had gotten Fern a pair of knock-off
Nike tennis shoes—size 8 wide, with Velcro—on his last trip to
China. Fern could use socks, sports bras, and a new hat, Sally said.
"Her favorite color is purple."

"Purple?" I asked.

"Purple is the color of royalty," Sally said. "And Fern says her
mother raised her to be a princess."

Sally seemed in awe of Fern. For Christmas she had given her a
piece of sheet music. "I knew that Fern would only appreciate
something really difficult to play," she said. "So I got the music with
the most notes on it." She particularly enjoyed hearing Fern's stories
about the trips she took with my grandparents to Italy and Israel.
"Did you know that Fern can count to ten in Italian?" Sally said.
"Or that her Hebrew name is Alana?"

I didn't.

Then Sally made a request that took me by surprise. "Do you or
any of your relatives have any photographs from Fern's past?"

"A few," I said.

"Could you put them together in an album for her?"

Like my other relatives, I had believed that the past was toxic for
Fern, that the memories it triggered would upset her. But Sally said,
"Fern has so much pride in her past, who she is, her Jewishness,
that whenever she hears voices or hallucinates or gets scared, I try to

redirect her to talk about the old times, the good times, when she played the piano and met the Pope and had big family dinners at her parents' house."

"I'll talk with Pudge and my parents and see what I can put together for you," I said.

"Thank you," Sally said.

The past didn't necessarily enrage Fern; in the hands of someone like Sally, it calmed and soothed her.

AS SOON AS she rounded the bend in her wheelchair, Fern began shouting, "Lee Richard Kravitz. It's my nephew, everyone. Lee Richard is here."

I asked Sally if I could take Fern into the courtyard.

"Of course," she said.

"Permission to smoke?" Fern asked.

"Yes, you have my permission," Sally said.

As Sally slipped the burn-proof vest over her head, Fern winked at me and asked, "How do you like my velvet smoking jacket, Lee Richard?" as if it were a piece of haute couture from Paris.

"It's beautiful," I said. "And quite trendy."

"Quite trendy," she mimicked in delight. "My smoking jacket is quite trendy."

I wheeled her into the courtyard. Fern's mood darkened the second we were alone. "I'm so scared," she said. "Someone tried to kill me last night. She was standing over me with a pillow. She tried to suffocate me. I'm so scared."

"Did you recognize her?" I asked.

"She was dressed in white. She had blond hair. She ran away when I screamed. She was trying to kill me, Lee Richard. You have to get me out of here."

Later, after the terror passed, Fern told me that what scared her most was the thought of dying alone. "I hope that there's someone there with me when I die," she said softly. "Someone to hold my hand."

I reached over, held her hand, and hoped that someone would be by her side when that time came. Pudge had told me that Fern didn't care about her burial arrangements, that cremation would be fine for her. That didn't make sense to me. Fern was a Jew and Jews since Abraham had been expected to be buried in the sanctified grounds of a Jewish cemetery.

"And what would you like to happen *after* you die?" I asked her.

"I want to be buried next to my Gerald, Lee Richard. Jerry bought two plots—number 104A for him, number 104B for me. Please bury me next to my Gerald," she said.

The next morning I drove to Mount Olive Cemetery and asked the manager for the location of Jerry's grave. I also asked, "Did he buy a second plot?"

It was just as Fern had remembered. "Mr. Litt bought 104A for himself and 104B for Fern Darla Litt," he said. He pointed out the window: "Do you see that flag over there? Walk halfway down the path next to it and turn right at row number 104."

I followed the man's directions and within two minutes I was standing at Jerry's grave. His headstone read: GERALD SHALE LITT 1929–1991. Above his name were the words: BELOVED HUSBAND. Fern would like that.

BACK AT AURORA Manor, there was a good-natured dispute going on between Fern and one of the other residents, Marge, a woman who was blind.

"It's Groundhog Day," Fern said.

"No, it's August sixteenth," the blind woman countered. "Groundhog Day is in February."

"Then it's Lee Richard Day," Fern said as I walked into the courtyard. "My nephew is here to visit me. Meet Lee Richard, Marge."

"Hello, young man," she said as I went over and grasped her hand. "Fern has been so happy since you've been coming here."

Fern liked women's magazines, particularly ones that featured recipes, so I gave her the latest issues of *Family Circle*, *Ladies' Home Journal*, and *Bon Appétit*.

Then I said, "I visited Jerry's grave at Mount Olive this morning—and guess what, Fern? You were right." I showed her a series of photos that I had taken with my cell phone: the entrance to Mount Olive, the flag, Jerry's headstone, and the empty plot next to it. "Here's your plot. Number 104B, just as you told me."

Fern reached over to hug me. "Number 104B. Just as I said."

"Just as you said."

Anxious to change the subject, Marge said, "Fern played piano this morning. Didn't you, Fern?"

"Yes I did, Lee Richard. I played 'Clair de Lune,' Rachmaninoff's Concerto No. 2, and 'My Yiddishe Mama.'"

"You played 'My Yiddishe Mama?'" I said. "Wasn't that Nana Shirley's favorite song?"

"Yes it was, Lee Richard." And she sang, "I owe what I am today to that Yiddishe Mama so old and gray. To that wonderful Yiddishe Mama. Oh Yussell, yussell, yussell, la la la, la la la . . ."

I took a small tape recorder out of my pocket and asked her to sing the song again, which she did. Then I asked her to repeat the poem she had recited to me the last time I had seen her. "The one about walking with pleasure and then sorrow," I said.

Fern sat up straight in the wheelchair and cleared her throat. "Is it on?" she asked.

"Yes," I said.

She recited the poem as flawlessly as she had done before.

"That's a beautiful poem, Fern," Marge said. "Did you write it?"

"Yes," she said proudly. "Want to hear my new song?" Fern asked us.

"Of course," I said.

Like a jazz singer, Fern began snapping her fingers and shaking her head to the rhythm of "I'm lovely, I'm sexy, I'm lonely, and I need it. I'm lovely, I'm sexy, I'm lonely, and I need it," which made Marge and Sally, who had just entered the courtyard, guffaw in delight.

I explained that I was taping Fern singing the songs she had sung to me when I was young. "I want to play them for my kids."

"Permission to tape?" Fern asked Sally.

"Of course," Sally said.

"Permission to flick?" Fern said.

"Flick away," Sally said, and Fern tapped an ash from her cigarette onto the ground.

Marge used the interlude to advance her pet cause: "I really think you should get a rabbi to come here to visit Fern. The rest of us have priests and ministers. Fern should have a rabbi." Marge was Irish Catholic and proud of it, and she was related to a bishop. "Fern may be the only person of the Jewish faith here," she proclaimed, "but she should be able to see a rabbi."

When I said it was a wonderful idea and that I'd try to make it happen, Marge said, "Your nephew loves you, Fern. Do you know that? He really loves you."

By then, Fern was snapping her fingers to another song: "Oh, that St. Lou-ee woman, with her diamond rings . . . St. Lou-ee woman, with all her diamond rings . . . Stole that man of mine, by her apron strings."

I asked Fern to tell her niece and nephews about her dogs. She leaned closer to the tape recorder.

"Hi, kids," she said. "This is your great-aunt Fern. My dogs were Buffy, Skippy, and Pookie the Poodle. Buffy used to jump up and grab food from the table. She tore up sheets and took letters from the mailbox and once the mailman said, 'Get that goddamn dog away from me, or I'll get him arrested.'"

Fern sang song after song, and as her concert came to an end,

I kept thinking about how my father would have the time of his life if he could hear his sister singing these songs again.

THE DAYS BETWEEN mid-August, when I left Fern, and the beginning of November, when I planned on seeing her again, were redolent with meaning.

In late August I turned fifty-five years old and began to see my age everywhere I drove. The signs that said SPEED LIMIT 55 beckoned me to ponder the increasingly small number of years that remained before I hit sixty, seventy, seventy-five, or eighty. Should I count my years or my blessings?

I went for the blessings. Just before the market went bust, Elizabeth and I had moved our money out of stocks and into bonds and our kids from private schools into public ones. I had agreed to coach Ben's baseball team, which would give me great joy. A book that Elizabeth represented was inspiring Americans to build schools for Muslim girls in Pakistan. And aside from Elizabeth's mother, who was descending quickly into the hell of Alzheimer's disease, our family (knock on wood) was healthy.

Probably the biggest blessing was how good I was feeling about taking care of my first piece of unfinished business. The previous October I had lost my job and confidence. I felt terrible about myself and my life. A few months later I decided to spend an entire year tying up my loose ends. I started with Fern because I missed her and wanted to show her how I still cared. In April, I found her and also the part of myself that she valued. In July, Pudge visited her, completing a piece of his own unfinished business. And now, on my third visit, I would be giving Fern a birthday party.

I invited my parents, brothers, Trina, Pudge, and a few other cousins to the party. Due to illness, distance, or busyness, most couldn't attend. But several promised to send Fern a gift or card and Trina said she'd bring the cake.

A week before the party, I put together the scrapbook I had promised Sally. It included photos of Fern as a girl, at my parents' wedding,
and on her trips to Israel, Greece, and Rome with my grandparents.
After I arrived in Cleveland, I went straight to a store that sold
Judaica and bought her an electric menorah, a 2009 calendar from
the Jewish Museum in Amsterdam, and two CDs of Jewish holiday
music.

Then, on the morning of November fourth, I drove out to Aurora
Manor with my bag full of birthday gifts. I arrived at eleven A.M.
The dining room was empty. But in the room next to it, I saw a
wonderful sight. Fern was sitting at a table surrounded by Allison,
Sally, Trina, and Trina's daughter Robyn. The cake Trina had brought
said, "Happy Birthday, Fern." There were flowers from Pudge and a
framed photograph of my cousin Debbie and her kids. Fern had
already started opening gifts: a down jacket and new sports bra from
Trina, a pair of tennis shoes from the staff. And Alice, her best friend
at Aurora Manor, was sitting next to her, waving a purple birthday
balloon.

I took out the CDs, calendar, and menorah from the bag and
presented them to Fern. Then I said, "Here's something I think you'll
really like," and placed the scrapbook of memories on the table in
front of her.

As she leafed through the scrapbook, I took a photo of Fern surrounded by friends and family, the people who loved her. I was
particularly pleased when Trina said that she and Robyn would try
to visit Fern once a week. In the parlance of my Jewish culture, I
had done a mitzvah. I felt encouraged by my success with Fern to
take care of the rest of my unfinished business, to see where other
journeys would take me.

"Time for cake," Trina said. There were six big candles and seven
little ones representing every decade and year of Fern's life. We
helped Fern blow them out, then wheeled her to the piano. The first
song Fern played was Claude Debussy's "Claire de Lune." Both she

and the piano were out of tune. But to my ears, it was the most
beautiful rendition of the song I had ever heard.

By then a crowd had gathered around the piano and Fern began
playing her other all-time favorites, "Yiddishe Mama" and "Hatikvah." When I had taped her humming "Hatikvah" on a previous
visit, she stopped in the middle of the song and said, "Top secret,
top secret," as if singing the song would bring dozens of anti-
Semites out of the woodwork. But today she played the song all the
way to the end and shouted, "Shalom!" The rest of us joined in.
"Shalom!" we shouted back.

It was like those Friday nights of another era when my parents
were young and beautiful and we'd stand behind Fern and her baby
grand in my grandparents' sumptuous living room, the entire family
singing "Climb Ev'ry Mountain," "Edelweiss," "The Sound of Music," "Fiddler on the Roof," "You'll Never Walk Alone," and "Those
Were the Days." I wished that Pudge was here, and my father.

Yes, Aunt Fern, it's a long story. But we are writing it together
at last.

CHAPTER TWO   # I'm So Sorry for Your Loss
Making a Condolence Call

ON THE MORNING of January 19, 2007, I came across one of the saddest newspaper stories I had ever read. On page two of the *New York Times*, next to the headline AMBUSH KILLS AN AMERICAN TEACHING DEMOCRACY IN IRAQ, there was a photo of a beautiful and vigorously alive young woman.

As a young man I would have fallen in love with her at a glance— with her blond pageboy, her blue eyes, and her engaging smile. It was easy to imagine this idealistic young woman teaching democracy in a war-torn country but impossible to imagine her dead.

My heart quickened even more when I saw her name. Andrea Parhamovich was the daughter of Andre Parhamovich, who had been the star right fielder on the baseball team I helped pitch to an Ohio state championship almost forty years ago. Comprised of pro hopefuls from all over Cleveland, the GO team was full of cocky tough guys—except for Andre, who made miraculous catches in the outfield and banged out game-winning hits without boasting. You could never imagine Andre dogging it or picking on a younger player like me the way some players did; he was too busy hustling from the dugout to the batter's box, from first base to second base, from the bench to his position in right field, joyously playing the game he loved.

I had not seen Andre since our summer of glory. But when I realized that the twenty-eight-year-old woman in the photo was his daughter, I lost it. I cried and cried as if my own daughter had been ambushed by Sunni insurgents in Iraq. Before that day I had no idea that Andi, as she was called, even existed. Now everything sad, raw, and unresolved in my life—my grandmother's death, 9/11, the cancer ravaging a friend's body—seemed bound up with her death. And that feeling worsened when I sat down to write Andre a condolence card and could only summon up excuses not to write him: How could I say "I'm sorry" to someone who had suffered so great a loss? Wasn't it selfish to intrude on his grief? Would Andre even remember me?

Elizabeth didn't buy any of my reasons for not reaching out to Andre. "Just write something," she said. "And send it. He'll appreciate the thought." My wife spoke from experience: Her brother had been killed by a drunken teenager just as his life was starting to make sense to him. Elizabeth also spoke from her knowledge of me. "You always find an excuse to procrastinate," she said, listing the five things that day I had promised but failed to do.

But I couldn't. Something much larger than my usual procrastination had attached itself to the condolence card, making it that much harder to write. That huge something was the immensity of death itself.

For the next three days, while riding the subway, watching television, editing a story, playing with the kids, and trying to fall asleep, I composed condolences in my mind that I either forgot or discarded. "Dear Andre: I don't know if you remember me . . ." "Dear Andre: When I read about Andi . . ." "Dear Andre: It has been nearly forty years since I last saw you . . ." Everything I wrote felt either stilted or trivial.

BY THEN THE story of Andi's death had been broadcast around the world. Ann Curry of the *Today* show said that Andi represented "the best of America." CBS News's Kellie Martin said she "seemed to have rocket fuel in her veins to make her life count."

Andi's ambitions had been far larger than the small Ohio town where she was raised. After graduating college, she worked for Governor Jane Swift of Massachusetts, Miramax Films, and Air America, the liberal radio network. Her goal was to become White House press secretary and eventually to run for Congress.

It was Andi's relationship with Michael Hastings, a Baghdad correspondent for *Newsweek*, that made her death even more tragic. They had planned to elope to Paris on Valentine's Day; just days before she died, Andi had e-mailed Michael her ring size.

In interview after interview, Michael described Andi with the same adjectives everyone else used: "She was beautiful. Funny. Intuitive. Really brilliant. And a bit of a nut."

"She was a little girl with big dreams," said her sister Marci.

And she was Andre's little girl. According to several news reports, Andre, who was identified as a former baseball and football coach, would break down and cry whenever he heard Andi's name. In a press conference outside the Parhamovich home, Marci's husband, Joe, said that Andre couldn't understand why thirty Sunni insurgents had targeted his peace-loving daughter with all that hatred and deadly force. Throughout the press conference, Andre stood sobbing in the background, his head hung low.

I GRIEVED DEEPLY for Andre's daughter. So why, nearly eighteen months after her death, did I still include a condolence card to Andre on my list of unfinished business?

There was my litany of doubts, of course, and my lifelong tendency to procrastinate. There was my fear of not knowing how to deal with another person's grief, of being inappropriate or wrong. But mainly there were the pressures and stressors of daily life, which made nothings seem like more than they were and pushed the important things aside.

That whole first week after I heard about Andi's death my thoughts were with her and Andre. But then I'd get lost in some sort of "crisis."

I recall how one afternoon I was summoned to the office of the publisher of the magazine I edited. He handed me a manuscript from a friend of his who had never written an article before. "You'll want to finish editing this by tomorrow morning," he said as he grabbed his briefcase and overcoat and headed for the train. "I would never ask you to do this unless I thought it would make a great article. Now remember, he isn't a writer." When he said this, with the elevator shutting in my face, I knew that the article I was about to edit for the next six hours would never see the light of day; I would show it to him on Friday and his whim to publish his friend's story would have passed.

Then, on Monday afternoon, as happened every Monday afternoon, the art director barged into my office to remind me of my failure, in his eyes, to meet the magazine's deadlines. "The designers don't have headlines," he shouted. "Without headlines, they can't design their stories." The editors came in to complain that the stories the art director was shouting about weren't due for another two weeks: How could they write headlines for stories they had not read?

There were other smaller crises too: How would we get from the country to the city in time for Caroline's piano recital? There was a draft in the house: Did I need to get the living room windows insulated with plastic? Would our dental insurance cover Noah's braces? If not, would we need to take out a loan?

Each of these crises, alone and in succession, kept me from writing a condolence card to Andre. It was the universal quandary: Modern life, with its distractions and pressures, made it extremely hard to find the time to deal with the issues that were most important in our lives—here, truly the most important, death and dying, and reaching out to a relative or friend in his suffering. The condolence card dropped to the bottom of my to-do list. It would stay there until I lost my job and decided to dedicate myself to completing my unfinished business.

BY THE TIME I finally saw Andre—June 17, 2008, at a nightclub in New York City—a year and a half had passed. During that time my daughter, Caroline, had reached puberty, discovered e-mail, and just that week been the recipient of a good-bye party at the school she'd attended since kindergarten. She had been looking forward to her new school—"It will mean more friends and more e-mail addresses," she said—but all of a sudden her typically cheery nature seemed to sour. At her going-away party, Caroline's two best friends had made a big deal out of not signing her yearbook. I had never seen my happy-go-lucky girl so sad.

It wasn't hard to decipher what was really going on: Caroline's friends felt rejected because she was about to leave them, and Caroline was more nervous than she could admit about changing schools. Elizabeth and I knew that pointing this out to our daughter would have made things worse; Caroline needed a hug from us, not a lecture. Also, she'd be over this particular hurt in a few days. Still, as I walked into The Cupping Room Cafe to see Andre, I thought, "I'd do anything I could to absorb my daughter's pain; what must it feel like to be Andre?"

THE CLUB WAS buzzing with celebrities and activity. Andi would have turned thirty that day and her friends and family were using the occasion to stage a benefit for the Andi Foundation, which gave out scholarships and internships to young women who were interested, as Andi had been, in pursuing a career in politics or the media.

It wasn't hard to find Andre in this crowd of artists and activists. Andre was the pale and paunchy fifty-something sitting alone in the back of the club, hunched over a table, staring down at his folded hands.

When she was thirty-two, the woman who had been my high school girlfriend was killed in an auto accident just days before her wedding. Those of us who had come to see Joyce married ended up burying her. I'll always remember the look on her father's face as they lowered her coffin into the grave: distracted, empty, devoid of feeling. It was clear he would never be okay.

And that's how Andre looked sitting alone at the table, like a man broken beyond repair.

I walked over to him and put my hand on his shoulder.

"Hi, Andre," I said. "I'm Lee Kravitz. You knew me years ago as Ricky."

"Ricky Kravitz. From the GO team. I remember your fastball," he said, without looking up. "Thanks for coming."

"I brought you something," I said. It was the one news clipping I still had from our championship season. It was dated Thursday, July 31, 1969, and headlined GO WINS CONNIE MACK.

Andre took the article and read it aloud: " 'GO is a storied name in Connie Mack circles, with a long list of present and past stars,' " he began. " 'Its graduates include this season's American League All-Star third baseman, Sal Bando of the Oakland A's.'

"Says here we won twenty-four of twenty-five games that season," he went on. "Not bad. Not bad at all."

Then Andre pointed to the man who stood in the middle of our team picture. "What a mean-assed motherfucker," he said with a scowl.

Coach Richie was GO's dictator of a manager. He had a crooked grin, shifty eyes, and a suspicious, calculating mind. If you were late to practice by even a minute, he'd make you run ten laps. If he saw you walking and not sprinting from the parking lot to the field, you'd be off the team.

And heaven help you if you missed one of Richie's signs. Richie was the only coach in America who used colored cardboard squares for signs. He'd stand like a Navy Signal Corps officer in the box at third base, flashing red, blue, green, blue, blue, which meant steal on the third pitch, or red, red, blue, green, red, which meant bunt and steal. If you missed a sign or got one wrong, he'd scream and kick dirt at you for the rest of the game.

During my best game that summer, I struck out nine players in a row, including Mike Easler, who would later star with the Pittsburgh Pirates, Boston Red Sox, and New York Yankees. During my final game, I threw out my arm on a curve ball—an injury that ended my pitching career. What made my disappointment even worse was Richie's response. He told me to take off my uniform and give it to a player he'd just drafted for the regionals. For the rest of that game I sat on the bench in the new player's baggy street clothes.

After I shared this memory with Andre, he offered his own Richie story. "In the state championship game I went two for three and got the winning hit," he said. "Know how that bastard thanked me? He benched me."

BY THEN THE festivities had begun. Rachel Maddow, an Air America anchor, got knowing laughs when she described how Andi would use her small-town charm to get everyone at the station, including Al Franken, to do her bidding. Andi's two nieces, Abby and Kayla, talked about their aunt in the present tense, as if she were still alive to play with them and twist their hair into braids. Ann Curry noted how the Parhamovich family was representative of the sacrifice that so many American families were making as the Iraqi war raged on. And Andre, getting more and more glum, just stared at his hands.

To cheer him up, I reported some information I'd uncovered earlier that week when I Googled everyone on the GO team to see if any of them had done anything of interest with their lives. They had. Five of our teammates had been drafted into the big leagues, four had become coaches, and one had become an ump.

I also had information on some of the guys who didn't go on in baseball. Al Zdesar, our star pitcher, became a college football referee, and Tom Dybzinski, our leading hitter, was a letter carrier.

"Wasn't Tom's brother Jerry the guy who lost the 1984 American League Championship for the White Sox when he ran past second base?" Andre asked.

"Yup, same guy," I said. "And you wouldn't believe what Mike Gaski is doing." Mike was one of the more lackluster players on the team. "Mike Gaski is head coach at the University of North Carolina at Greensboro and he's president of USA Baseball."

"No kidding," Andre said.

"Mike runs the U.S. Olympic baseball team. And his son Matt was drafted this year by the San Diego Padres," I said.

"No kidding," Andre said again.

It was clear that all this unsolicited information was putting Andre in a better mood, as was the music of a young singer/composer from Texas named Carrie Rodriguez, whose jazzy country tunes got him tapping his feet.

Carrie's band ended the set with a song called "St. Peter's." "I wrote it for a friend of mine who was killed while riding his bicycle," she said. "His name was Andy, too."

Then she sang:

It's been not . . . not yet a year
Time goes by and disappears
As for me, I'm doing fine
Just need some help from time to time.

I looked over at Andre. His feet were still and his body was shaking. He was not—would he ever be?—okay.

* * *

AS I RODE the subway uptown to 110th Street, I thought about Andre. I couldn't articulate exactly how or why, but I felt that a strong intimacy had taken root. And it was strange. Andre had been shattered emotionally and yet we'd steered clear of the pain; we just talked baseball.

"How did it go?" Elizabeth asked as I walked into the apartment.

"We talked baseball," I said. "I didn't say how sorry I was for his loss. We never even mentioned Andi's name."

"How did that make you feel?"

"Good," I said. "I can't put my finger on it, but I feel close to Andre."

"You gave each other what you needed," Elizabeth said.

"I guess so," I said.

THE NEXT DAY I wrote Andre what he probably already knew:

Dear Andre:

I was deeply honored to spend so much time with you at the benefit. When I first read of Andi's death and realized that she was your daughter, I felt sad for days. I wanted to reach out to you but didn't know if you'd even remember me. Then life and the pressure of putting out the magazine took over and I never followed through on what I'd intended. That's why it was so important for me to attend the benefit.

Literally hours after I sent that e-mail, I received a heartfelt note that Andre must have written just after the benefit:

Hi Lee. I really enjoyed talking to you! You helped me to keep control of my emotions and to get through the evening in a positive manner.

Andre's sign-off—"Remember to keep sports enjoyable"—struck a particularly resonant chord.

That's because my father had been one of those dads who believe that sports is the be-all and end-all, life's great teacher and motivator. When I was five years old, he threw a ball ten feet into the air so that it fell directly on my head. While I was crying from pain, he said, "See, son, it hardly hurts," which made me cry even more. In the world according to Harry, pain built character.

Even the sadistic Coach Richie chastised my father for being dangerously overinvolved in my sports career. Whenever I took the mound for GO, my father would stand behind the backstop and signal the pitches he thought I should throw. If I didn't throw a pitch he'd ordered, say a slider, and the batter hit what I did throw, say a fastball, he'd broadcast his rightness—and my stupidity—to the crowd: "See, he should have listened to me. He should have thrown a slider."

In one game I got so unnerved by my father's commands for me to throw The Big One, by which he meant a curve ball, that Coach Richie banished him to the parking lot for the rest of the game and season. The lesson was lost on my father. If you looked toward the parking lot while I was pitching, you would have seen him sitting on the hood of our Chevy, motioning for me to throw The Big One—The Big One, he'd gesture again—then shaking his head disdainfully when I did not.

Andre had known my dad back then. And he'd known the pressure we felt during those games. Shortly after the benefit for Andi, as we began our e-mail exchange, I shared with him an e-mail my father had sent to me. The context for the e-mail was this: Ben had made his league's all-star team but the game wouldn't be played until two weeks after the season was over. My father, who lived twelve hundred miles away in Florida, was concerned that his grandson would not be sharp for the game.

So he wrote:

It is 'very important' that you do not allow Benjamin to 'lose his desire to perform well' during this 'waiting period,' Lee! 1) You should practice his 'Form & Control Regimens' when it is 'not raining'; also his 'Fielding Regimens.' 2) You should 'keep him loose' both in 'Body' and 'Mind' so that he will take the Field 'believing in himself' and not be 'worrying about any rumored abilities' of the 'Opposition' that he will be facing. 3) This is Benjamin's 'initiation' into the 'Real World of Athletic Competition' and it is 'very important' that he emerges from the experience in the proper frame of mind.

I had a viscerally bad reaction to my father's e-mail. It struck me as just one more example of his motioning me to throw The Big One—The Big One—only this time from twelve hundred miles away. I presumed that he was pushing me to push my son as hard as he had pushed me, and I resented it. I thought Andre would agree.

"Wow! Your dad sure takes baseball seriously," Andre e-mailed back. But instead of joining me in my mockery of my father's excesses, he wrote, "I bet he'd get a big kick seeing *you* coach a team." It was the first of several insights from Andre that would challenge my view of my father, the world, and myself.

I HAD ALWAYS wanted to coach Ben's team, but I had dismissed that idea for two reasons. First, when I worked in publishing, I did not want to commit myself to anything that might be perceived as an activity that competed with my job. Second, I remembered what it was like to have a father as a coach. Mine was extraordinary, probably the best I ever had, but there was always the sense, among my teammates and myself, that he was either favoring me or being harder on me, which was an uncomfortable burden for me to shoulder.

The more I thought about Andre's suggestion, however, the less my excuses made sense. It had been more than seven months since I lost my job. And my son could more than hold his own; if I started him at shortstop, no one could accuse me of favoring him.

I volunteered to coach Ben's team.

Dear Andre:

With your encouragement, I have just become the proud manager of a team of 11-year-olds. I am looking forward to this challenge but it now strikes me that I have forgotten how to run a practice. I could use a refresher course on drills and also a pregame warmup that will keep my team focused and motivated. Can you help?

He wrote back:

Hi Lee. Your e-mail brings a smile to my face—and there have not been many smiles since Andi's death. I am eager to teach you some drills and a warmup.

That week I headed to Cleveland.

ANDI'S BEST FRIEND was scheduled to arrive in Cleveland on the same day, so I told her that I would pick her up at the airport and give her a lift to Perry. With her hipster eyeglasses, flowing skirt, ankle tattoo, and sandals, Jaime struck me as an appealing mix of New York career girl, wild child, and lost soul. When I greeted her at baggage claim, she seemed distracted, as if her body had arrived but not her mind.

"Andi was my best friend . . . ever," she told me as we headed eastward on I-90 through downtown Cleveland and along the shore of Lake Erie. They would talk about politics and boy-friends, she said, but also about stuff that would have struck most of their Air America colleagues as odd, including angels and the fact that they had been sisters in at least four previous lives. They also believed that the spirits of the dead communicate with their loved ones.

"We were always imagining the other side and then, all of a sud-den, Andi was there, on the other side herself," Jaime said ironi-cally, and softly, as the fast-food and auto-repair shops along I-90 gave way to cornfields. "I remember times when I had the feeling that Andi wouldn't be on earth very long. She was so fearless and courageous and good. Sometimes I get signs that she's watching over me or reaching out to me."

Jaime was traveling to Perry to help Andre and his wife, Vicki, celebrate Abby's birthday. Abby, their granddaughter, was going to be nine. Andi had been the fun, cool aunt who brought Abby and her older sister, Kayla, gifts from exotic places. As Abby and Kayla grew up, Andi would have been the one who tended to their hurts, listened to their dreams, and prodded them to make the most of their lives. This would now be Jaime's role.

I could appreciate how Jaime felt. In the months following 9/11, one of my dearest friends died of stomach cancer after a cruel and dignity-destroying illness. Elizabeth and I never articulated it to Phil, but as soon as it was clear he would die, we knew that we would watch over Tracy and his three kids for the rest of our lives. We wanted to make sure that Phil's memory and spirit remained strong. It was one of the few ways we could keep him alive in our own hearts and come to terms with his death.

Now that Phil's kids were older, though, it made me sad that he wasn't around to celebrate the remarkable convergence of his genes with their emerging selves. I wondered aloud whether the sight of Abby and Kayla, who Jaime described as being a "mini-Andi," would make her sad.

"Not at all," Jaime said. "What worries me, sometimes, is seeing Andre and Vicki. Grief can be competitive. If you've loved someone as much as I loved Andi, you can't imagine anyone being sadder at her loss or grieving her more deeply.

"I used to resent Andre and Vicki for their grief. But I'm getting over that. I'm learning that we each experience grief in our own deep way, which makes it easier for me to both comfort and be comforted by them."

A MILE FROM Perry, two huge white towers came into view. They were shaped like hourglasses and billowed white smoke. They reminded me of the Twin Towers at the World Trade Center, how they dominated the cityscape before 9/11. Yet the towers looming over Perry looked out of place, like rockets that had just crashed into a cornfield.

"That's them," Jaime said as she saw the towers. And then I remembered that these imposing structures were the reason Andre had moved to Perry in the first place. Because they created nuclear waste, their construction had spurred protests that made the national nightly news. In response, the state of Ohio funneled millions of extra dollars into Perry's public school system, which became one of the best in the nation. Andre didn't like living so close to a nuclear power plant, but when it came to raising his kids in Painesville, with its decrepit and crumbling schools, or in Perry, the choice was clear.

We turned right down Townline Road, which separated Perry from the town of Madison, and then took another right back toward Perry. The road was lined by hundreds of acres of flowering plant nurseries. I turned left into the driveway of a wooden farmhouse. Three generations of Parhamoviches converged on our car: Andre and Vicki, their daughter Marci and her husband, Joe, and their granddaughters, Abby and Kayla, who ran to Jaime for hugs. Before I could say hello, Andre took my arm and pulled me into the yard. "Let's get to work," he said.

Over the next two hours, Andre taught me a pregame warm-up, several fielding drills, and a variety of ways to build hitting skills using Wiffle balls, Fungo Bats, and plastic golf balls. Abby and Kayla wanted to join us, but he shooed them away.

Andre's "singular focus" was also apparent at dinner, where he only seemed interested in talking about baseball and how young people today have an insufficient work ethic.

Both Jaime and his family indulged Andre and avoided any mention of Andi. My friend, it turned out, was a great baseball mentor, but he was an emotional mess, which saddened me because I could only imagine how shattered I would be if one of my own children died.

WHEN I RETURNED to New York, I began to prepare for our team's first practice. I wanted to get across the importance of hustling, being alert, and playing to the best of your potential. We were going to stress fundamentals, I would say, and we'd play our hardest to win because winning is a lot more fun than losing. I rehearsed my spiel in front of Ben and Caroline, who liked the general drift but said I needed to be more concise and smile more. To drive the point home, Ben said, "Don't be Grandpa Harry."

"This is making me nervous," I wrote to Andre.

"The reason you're nervous, my friend, is that you're coaching your own children," he wrote back. "I felt the same way when I coached my kids. You're concerned what the other players and their parents will think, so you become tougher on your children. It never works. Treat them like you would any other player."

After our first game—a 5–1 victory over Rhinebeck—I gave Andre a detailed report: "Our pitching was great but our hitting was abysmal." The next game didn't go as well, and we lost. "I know it's only Little League," I wrote Andre. "But I'm depressed."

"That's the nature of the beast," he wrote back. "No matter what

level you coach, a defeat feels like you've personally failed your
team. You can't let defeat consume you."

The fact is, it did consume me. I must have spent two hours com-
piling every conceivable statistic about the first two games—runs
scored and batted in, slugging percentage, on-base percentage,
strikeout-to-walk ratio—as if these numbers, like tea leaves, would
reveal the future path to victory.

One statistic stood out. In the first two games the players on my
team struck out a total of twenty-nine times—almost two and a
half times an inning. As Ben and Noah like to say, we sucked.

In an e-mail to Andre I offered my own analysis—the best hitters were swinging too hard and the worst hitters weren't swinging
at all—and asked for his advice.

He wrote back:

> Your sluggers just want to crush the ball. Ask them: "What's
> more important, swinging as hard as you can and missing or
> making contact and getting a hit?"
>
> As for the second problem, the players who aren't striding into
> the pitch are afraid of it. Remind them to stand close to the plate
> and on the "balls" of their feet. And be sure to show them exactly
> what you mean; otherwise, they'll never get it.

In our 25–5 win over Poughkeepsie, the kids who were over
swinging made contact and felt great after they got hits. So did
some of our more timid hitters, who swung and eked out singles.
Only one player, our starting pitcher, got rattled—and I noticed
how he kept looking at his father after every pitch, as if he expected
to be reprimanded. "What should I do?" I e-mailed Andre.

"Shower that young man with praise," he wrote. It was exactly
the opposite of what this son of Harry had been doing.

* * *

OVER TIME MY friendship with Andre deepened. I e-mailed him far more than any other friend and gleaned nuggets of wisdom from our daily back-and-forth about Ben's baseball team. The intimacy of our baseball talk encouraged me to probe deeper into the one area of his life we didn't discuss: his grief over Andi. "Is it getting any easier?" I wrote. "I would really like to know." When he wrote back that he and Vicki discussed the matter and would like to share what they had learned about grief with me, I booked a flight to Cleveland.

I met them at Marci's home in Perry, and then accompanied them to a nearby park that looked out over Lake Erie. "This is my special place," Andre told me. "I come here every day to be alone with my thoughts and," he added softly, "to talk with Andi."

Andre's confession startled me; in the five months we'd been e-mailing each other, he barely mentioned his daughter's name. Now, it turned out, he had been talking with Andi almost every day and having what Jaime and Vicki call "Andi moments"— encounters that defy reason and surprise them with joy.

"You'll never believe this," he said as he pulled me toward a bench facing the lake. "A few weeks ago I found out that I could dedicate one of these benches to Andi. It drove me crazy because I couldn't figure out which bench it should be, under which tree?

"And guess what?" he said, pointing to a word that's barely legible. "No, closer," he commanded. The word, etched in blue ink, said "Andrea," Andi's birth name. "I have no idea who put it there," he told me, "but I'll bet that Andi had something to do with it. Andi and her angels."

To explain why he was so sure, Andre described another cloudy day in September when he came to the park feeling defeated by life, hopeless. Then all of a sudden the sun broke through the clouds and he was enveloped in what he calls an "indescribable" warmth. "It was a feeling of complete contentment, bliss, serenity, and peace of heart, all wrapped into one," he confided. "Vicki likes to think it was Andi giving me a hug. I like to think it was Andi saying, 'Don't worry. I'm still here, Dad. I'm okay.'"

Which is not to say that the pain was gone, or the anger. If Andre came face-to-face with any of the thirty Sunni insurgents who ambushed and murdered Andi, he would strangle them until they were dead.

I wondered, Did Andre ever blame the man who presided over the U.S. war effort for Andi's death? Was he angry at George W. Bush?

"No," Andre said. "It was Andi's choice to go. She knew exactly what she was getting into."

How about God? Did Andre, a Catholic, ever blame or question God?

"Yes I do."

He told me about a conversation he had with God less than ten feet from where we were standing. "Right there, in front of that tree, I shouted, 'Why have you done this to me?'" he said. "Then a voice inside my brain said, 'Andre, I haven't forsaken you. I've been by your side the whole time.'"

That response quieted Andre for a couple of months. Then a week before my visit, he lost faith again. He bolted from a church during the wedding of a family friend. "The bride had blond hair, just like Andi," he explained. "And I remembered how Andi was going to marry Michael in Paris, on Valentine's Day. I couldn't bear it. So I ran out of the church and fell to my knees. I shouted, 'You took away my daughter, my precious daughter. Why, God? Why?'

"And then I heard that voice again. It said, 'Seek ye first the Kingdom of God, and his righteousness, and all these things shall be added unto you.' And I said, 'I don't want your riches; I want my daughter back.'"

By temperament and by necessity, Vicki had had an easier time coping with Andi's death. "After Andi died, I had a role. I had to be strong for Andre, strong for Marci, and strong for our two boys.

The boys were only seventeen at the time," she told me. "They could have dropped out, got into drugs, or even taken their lives because they didn't want to deal with Andi's death. I had to be there day and night for them. I could not break down."

Vicki urged Andre and the boys to go into therapy, which they finally did. While Andre continued to rage at God, Vicki embraced him.

"I wouldn't have been able to be as strong as I've been if I didn't have faith in God," she told me. "But I must admit that I talk to Andi more than God now. I talk to her all day long.

"And right now, she's telling me that we better get back to Marci's house for dinner."

As we walked toward the parking lot, Andre told me how he dreams of traveling to Iraq. "I want to go to Baghdad with Michael after the war ends. I want to be there on January 17, the day Andi died. I want to stand as a free American on the street corner where she was killed and know that Andi didn't die in vain."

And Vicki?

"If that ever happens, if the war ever ends, I'll stay home," she said. "Seeing where Andi died would just upset me. What comforts me is the fact that my daughter felt strong and confident enough while she was alive to live her life the way she wanted. Andre misses his little girl. I miss the woman she would have become."

WHENEVER I FLY in an airplane there's a moment at takeoff when I contemplate the possibility of my own death and the impact it will have on my wife and kids. It's an unnerving thought, and I put it to rest by tightening my seat belt and taking a deep breath.

This time, though, it wasn't my own death that concerned me as we took off from Cleveland to New York; what worried me was the possibility that Ben, Noah, or Caroline could be killed while I was airborne. That thought—the possibility of losing the only people in the world whose lives meant more to me than my own—filled me with a sorrow so deep that it took my arrival home and the sight of my kids to end it: "Daddy, Daddy, did you bring us any gifts?"

The next day I received a note from Andre that said, "Please read the attached letter. It means a lot to me."

The letter had been written by U.S. senator George Voinovich after Andi died. The senator and his wife had experienced their own terrible loss. In 1979, a month before he was elected Cleveland's mayor, their nine-year-old daughter, Molly, was struck and killed by a van.

"We know that there will be difficult days ahead as you adjust to the loss of Andi," Voinovich wrote. "Janet and I have never completely adjusted to Molly's death. Every so often, without warning, a flood of memories will return. You will think that you cannot make it through another day. Trust me," he concluded. "You will."

Why did the senator's letter mean so much to Andre?

"When I think I can't go on," Andre said, "I remember the phrase, 'Trust me, you will.'"

A few days later Andre told me about a woman in his bereavement group whose oldest son had been killed five years earlier in a car accident. "She was just learning to live with his loss," Andre said. "So guess what happens? Her youngest son gets killed in a car crash. I feel terrible for her. For weeks I've been wallowing in self-pity. Now I'm going to stop. I bet if you look around the room—look around any room—you'll find a person with a bigger problem or in worse pain."

For the last few months Andre had been looking for an answer to his grief; now, it seemed, he had found it.

"When you grieve for a child, it's like you're always swimming through a sea of sadness," he explained. "Some days you swim at sea level and other days you swim above it. But most days you swim below sea level and struggle for air. It's on those days that you get lifted up by the kindness of others."

If there is an antidote to grief, he was discovering, it is compassion—the kindness that others show to you and that you show to others.

Wordsworth called it:

That best portion of a good man's life
His little, nameless, unremembered acts of kindness and of love.

I had been the recipient of some of those acts after I lost my job. At a time when I grieved the loss of my identity and felt shat upon, some of the people I considered colleagues and friends dropped me like a rock or kept a cold distance—leaving me with the feeling that our relationships had been based solely on what I could do for them. There were other people, however, who made an effort to thank me and wish me well. A person I barely knew offered to help me pack; another helped me transfer my contact list and other files I might find useful from my computer. These gestures touched me deeply. And as Andre had come to understand, they made me more likely to lend my own "best portion" to others.

Andre will never be entirely okay. He'll battle depression, argue with God, and question life's meaning for the rest of his life. At times he'll get short with Vicki or his grandkids and then realize, upon reflection, that it's not them he's mad at; it's the fact that he'll never see Andi again.

Andre's suffering has consumed him, but it has also made him a kinder, more compassionate man.

Lately he's been talking about a boy in his first-grade gym class whose younger brother died a year ago from a bacterial infection. Josh seemed fine for a year, but in the last few weeks he'd been acting out in class and asking questions like "Why did my brother die after the doctor told us he wouldn't?"

"I could see that Josh was really angry today," Andre wrote me. "So I made a point of shooting hoops with him. I let him beat me in a game of one on one. He blocked all my shots. I could tell it made a huge difference—for me, too. I'm feeling good today."

And there is something else that Andre had been doing to manage his grief. Every Wednesday and on the seventeenth day of each month, he fasted. "It helps me to not take the suffering and pain that people like Andi and our veterans go through for granted," he said. "I fast for their families, too, for like my own, they are the walking wounded."

WHEN WE STARTED to correspond with each other after the benefit for the Andi Foundation, Andre would end his e-mails with the phrase "Your friend, Andre." Now he ends them with the phrase "LFL."

"You are only the 4th person to receive my text closing of LFL, which means 'Loyalty, Friendship and Love,'" he wrote me. "The other three are Jaime, Michael, and Paul Rieckhoff of the Iraq and Afghanistan Veterans of America organization."

The fact that I've become an LFL means a lot to Andre—and to me, too. I am honored by Andre's loyalty, friendship, and love and will be there for him whenever he needs me for as long as I live.

The unfinished business in this chapter began with my failure to send Andre a condolence card after his daughter's death. I had every intention of doing so, but I allowed doubts and deadlines to get in my way.

Going forward, I pledged to "just do it" whenever I found myself in a similar circumstance. As both Andre and Elizabeth told me, a statement as simple as "I'm sorry for your loss" can take the edge off a person's grief. A friendly ear or an hour of playing catch or shooting hoops can help a grieving person make it through another day.

But grief is only part of the story. The circle of compassion goes round and round, transforming every person who touches it. Take me. During this season of grieving and baseball with Andre, I had become a much more charitable son to my father. Unexpectedly, by reaching out to Andre in his suffering, I came away with a much richer relationship with my dad.

After every game, I would e-mail my father a report that included Ben's statistics and an account of my good and questionable coaching decisions. I could see, by the length of his responses, that he got a big kick out of my coaching, just as Andre had predicted.

I could visualize my father sitting in his study in Florida, waiting all day for my reports. Because he is deaf, my father's world is small, isolated, and quiet. But I could imagine the buzz in his study as he'd open my latest e-mail and call out to my mother to come into the room, quick, so he could tell her Ben's statistics and describe how he would never have sent the runner to third like I had done, unsuccessfully, on that one-out hit to the outfield.

"We had our last game today and beat Hyde Park 6–5," I wrote him. "So our final record was 4–2, with victories over three teams that almost always beat us.

"Ben batted .525 and was the team's leading pitcher, averaging over two strikeouts per inning. He only made one error all year, and made some over-the-shoulder catches at shortstop that thrilled the crowd."

Using brackets and a red font, my father wrote:

[Sounds (Pun) like your Children are making the most out of their 'Athletic Genes', Lee! It is 'very important' that you 'keep their Heads fitting in their Caps', however (if you 'understand what I mean')!]

In the long history of our relationship, I usually would have bristled at this advice. But this time I smiled. I gave my father full credit for being the source of my kids' athletic genes. And I wrote him that I understood exactly what he meant by the importance of keeping their heads from getting too large.

It meant that he was as proud of them as I was.

CHAPTER THREE

The Check Is in the Mail

Repaying a Long-Overdue Debt

OVER THIRTY YEARS ago I asked my friend John for six hundred dollars so that I could continue traveling with him and our friend Jim through India. Earlier that day, on the cow-clogged road from Allahabad, we had stopped to watch a naked, white-bearded sadhu prostrate himself in the direction of Varanasi, Hinduism's holiest city. It had been such a remarkable sight that we spent twenty minutes at the side of the road watching the pilgrim creep ahead, impervious to the lorries and rickshaws dodging him. First he would lie head-to-toe on the ground. Then he would reach out his arm and make a mark with a stubby piece of chalk. Then he would get up, take three steps, stand on the mark, bend down, and prostate himself again. It would be at least fifty more miles before the sun-scorched ascetic would reach Varanasi's temples and sacred ghats.

It took us only a few hours to get to Varanasi in our Land Rover that day. John and Jim went shopping for silk, while I wandered the narrow, winding lanes taking photographs. We met up later at Manikamika ghat, where the body of a Hindu Brahmin was being cremated on the steps leading down to the Ganges. It was here, on the banks of this most holy and polluted of rivers, witnessing a spectacle of fierce and unsettling beauty, that I asked John for the loan.

"I'm running out of rupees," I said. "Can you help me out? I'm dead broke."

"No problem," he said, as nonchalantly as one friend offering another a cigarette. John's father owned the biggest cattle-feed operation in eastern Colorado at the time, so money really wasn't a problem to him. "How much do you need?" he asked.

"Six hundred bucks," I said. "When we get back to the States, I'll send you a check."

I never did—not in 1977, when I returned to the States, nor by 2008, when I set out to attend to the unfinished business of my life.

At first it was because I didn't have the money. Then I needed whatever money I earned for rent. Then I needed it to pay off student loans. Then I needed it to move from Cleveland to New York to attend journalism school. Then, after journalism school, I needed it for rent and to pay off student loans again—and so on. I always seemed to live a hand-to-mouth life, where ends never quite met. The fact that John came from a wealthy family lessened the urgency I felt to pay him back.

But the debt kept nagging at me.

As the years went by, the six hundred dollars grew to six thousand in my mind. I assumed that John was angry at me for reneging on the loan. Periodically I'd resolve to contact him and settle my account, but I never did. It was stupid of me to let such a relatively small amount of money stand between me and a friend. And I paid a price for it. The older I got, the less I remembered about the most exciting adventure of my life. I wanted that trip to remain vivid in my mind for as long as possible, but I had burnt my bridge to one of the two people in the world who could help me remember it.

THE FACT THAT I had spent my first two years after college traveling through one of the roughest and most politically unstable regions in the world did not impress my wife or children. For one thing, my kids were just getting to the age when they could locate Iran, Afghanistan, and India on the map. Also, the idea that their father had once been an adventurer did not square with their picture of me as the guy who stayed home to work when they went on hikes and bike rides and to the beach with their mother.

In my kids' eyes, I was about as far as you can get from being Marco Polo or Christopher Columbus. It was Elizabeth who took them on fun adventures that broadened their horizons and showed them new worlds: skiing in Vermont, whale-watching on Cape Cod, the sheep-and-wool and garlic festivals in Upstate New York, a whole week once in London, England, going to museums, cathedrals, and plays. If I ventured anywhere, it was to Washington, Chicago, or L.A. on a business trip.

Elizabeth insisted that Noah take fencing lessons, Caroline try horseback riding, and Ben catch frogs and worms. In the summer, she taught the kids to swim and sail. In the fall, she jumped into the leaves with them. In the winter, she skated around the lake with them. Mom was game for anything; Dad, the wimp, was a drag.

Paying back John and ridding myself of the debt I owed him was a way to clear my conscience of baggage I didn't need to be carrying. But I also knew that it would be more than that. Like reconnecting with Andre or Aunt Fern, I sensed that it would be a way to reactivate a part of myself that had fallen dormant. Perhaps I could summon up my younger, more adventurous self and bring it into the present enough so that my kids might even notice.

FROM FEBRUARY UNTIL October 1976, Jim and John and I traveled overland from Tehran to Calcutta in a Land Rover we called Rosie. There was a civil war in the westernmost region of Pakistan, Indira Gandhi had just jailed most of her political opponents in India, the Russians were about to make their fateful decision to invade Afghanistan, and Iran's Ayatollah Khomeini was getting ready to depose the shah.

I wanted to remember the details of our trip through these strife-ridden countries and revive them in my own memory and imagination. Little by little over the years they had been slipping away.

Did we really almost starve to death when we got lost trying to follow Alexander the Great's route through southern Iran?

Did Pashtuns on horseback surround our Land Rover and shoot their rifles into the air as we climbed the Khyber Pass from Pakistan into Afghanistan?

Did the parasite that caused the dysentery that destroyed my digestive system come from the water buffalo milk I drank while talking politics with Ghous Bux Khan Mahar, the Pakistani tribal leader?

Only John or Jim would know for sure. And only they could confirm my recollection of July 4, 1976, when we celebrated our nation's bicentennial birthday at the U.S. embassy in New Delhi by riding on a giant hand-built ferris wheel powered by barefooted men in cotton loincloths. Or the time we hid our Land Rover behind some rocks and waded across the swirling river separating Nepal from Tibet less than one hundred yards away from a Red Chinese border guard. Or the day we spent twelve hours reassembling Rosie after Afghani and Iranian border guards dismantled her while searching for drugs and subversive literature.

Those would be wonderful stories to tell my children someday. But before I could, I would need to find John and pay back the six hundred dollars I owed him.

WHEN I LAST saw him, outside the Ataturk International Airport in Istanbul, John was headed to London to sell Rosie, our Land Rover. It was the first week of October in 1976. After he and Jim dropped me at the airport, I flew from Istanbul to Israel, where I spent six months harvesting bananas on a kibbutz.

From what I could discover through the Internet, John went back to Colorado that fall to attend law school. A few years later, he joined and became a partner at one of Denver's most prestigious law firms.

Because one of Elizabeth's brothers was also a lawyer in Denver, I asked him if he knew of John.

"I never met him," Jamie said. "But I certainly know of him. His office is two floors down from mine. We've probably shared the same elevator dozens of times. Small world."

Yes, small world. My brother-in-law specialized in collections law; two floors below him, an unwitting John was about to collect on the six hundred dollars I had owed him for thirty-three years. In the note I sent along with the check, I urged John to "employ the $600 however you would like — toward charity, a gift to your wife, or your own pleasure." As interest on the loan, I suggested that I fly to Denver and take him to dinner: "That way, we can catch up on our lives and remember Rosie," I wrote.

I waited for John's reply.

WHEN JIM INVITED me to travel with him and his buddy John to India, we had just graduated college and I had only one hundred dollars in the bank. I was clueless as to my immediate future, so Jim's plan fired me up and set me in motion. I worked the midnight cleanup shift at a plastics factory for three months to save the three thousand dollars Jim predicted I'd need for the trip. By then, he and John had bought Rosie in London and driven her to Istanbul.

When I got to England, it became even less likely that I'd ever catch up with them. I spent a month in London hanging out with a friend whose sister was a famous model there. Then I got an assignment to interview my hero, the French photographer Henri

Cartier-Bresson, in Paris. By then, John and Jim had driven from Istanbul to Tehran, where they were waiting for me.

In truth, I had cold feet: I had never traveled abroad before and I was beginning to internalize my parents' fears for my safety and question whether a trip to India would do anything to advance my life. Jim sensed my trepidation and wrote me a letter from Tehran that I will always treasure. It was dated January 11, 1976, and I've kept it all these years as a reminder to follow your heart as well as your head, particularly when the voices you hear in your head are those of your parents.

Dear Leebo,
Try to get to Istanbul as soon as you can. The best and cheapest way to get from Istanbul to Tehran is aboard what they call the Magic Bus, which leaves for the East two times a week and costs $23 for the Tehran leg. The booking office is located on Divan-yolu Caddesi in the area of town known as Sultanahmet, near the Blue Mosque.

There are a shit-load of young Americans, Germans, Italians and the like who are migrating towards Kabul, Katmandu and Krishna Consciousness these days. A lot of them look like they tripped once too often, but it's a mixed bunch and you can come across some pretty interesting stories, psychological defenses, aspirations, popular myths, revolutionary spirit, cynicism . . . a mosaic of this generation's existential nausea . . . fascinating stuff for an article or two.

If I were you, I wouldn't miss too much of the Iranian interlude—petrol is so inexpensive here we can afford to do a lot of truckin': 20 cents a gallon from the last report. Financially I'd say we have a floating ship. The Rover cost us $3800—a sizable chunk of the wallet, but since that covers the major expense, transportation, you should be alright. Our living expenses have been around $5 a day, and this is the most expensive country in Asia. By the way, Rosie, the Land Rover, is a beaute, complete with rooftrack, 4-wheel drive, and a front-mounted winch.

In the margins of Jim's letter, you can see the quick computation I made. At seven dollars a day for living expenses and petrol, I would be able to travel overland to India and back for a little more than one hundred days. If I sold an article or two, I might be able to eke out another two months on the road. By those calculations, I would be back in Cleveland by late summer or fall.

Jim's letter went on:

All I can say is that being on the road is its own kind of experience, unforgettable and unique. We've been from the whore houses of Istanbul to the tangerine groves of Bodrum to the Temple of the Oracle of Apollo. In Istanbul, John got himself arrested in the student riots that have been closing down the universities. Thieves pried one of Rosie's windows open and copped all of John's color film, my camera and tripod, our medical kit, and some camping gear. One humorous aspect, though—they also made off with a bag of paperbacks . . . our lightweights like *Finnegans Wake* and *Gravity's Rainbow* and other books easily grasped with your pocket Turkish-English Dictionary.

Jim's letter sold me on traveling to India: If I didn't join them, I would miss out on the trip of a lifetime. So I bought a ticket on the Orient Express from Paris to Istanbul and spent the next two days cuddling for warmth with two sixty-something Bulgarian women who were smuggling jeans they had bought in Paris for their grandchildren. With my shoulder-length hair, I got hassled at every border we crossed, but my Bulgarian friends succeeded in yanking me back on the train before the guards could pull me off. When we reached Sophia, their final stop, my protectors instructed me to hide the jeans they had bought under my seat. As the train left the station, I tossed the jeans out the window, into the arms of their waiting grandchildren.

Several hours later, the train arrived in Istanbul during the worst winter in modern Turkish history. Because of the snow and below-zero temperatures, I wouldn't be able to find a train headed to Tehran for another week. I ended up taking a room in a cheap Sultanahmet hotel, feebly heated by a single coal-fed radiator. To keep warm, I spent my days drinking coffee and smoking cigarettes at a local cafe. When the trains started running again, the trip from Istanbul to Tehran took three days longer than usual because of the snow and ice. My four cabinmates were members of a religious cult called Children of God, who threw apples and leaflets out the window whenever we passed through a new village and tried to convert me and the other men on the train. They called their conversion strategy "flirty fishing," which entailed sex that I thought best to decline. Before we reached Ankara, a passenger smoking a cigarette between cars told us that two Afghanis had been found frozen to death in one of the third-class cabins: It was *that* cold.

On the sixth day, we passed through dozens of mud villages and neared Tehran. From the train, we could see a white marble tower. The shah had built it five years earlier on the 2,500th anniversary of the Persian Empire. One of the Children—a pretty blond waif from Australia—tried to persuade me to stay on the train and accompany her and her friends to India. I got off. The taxi took me from the train station past gleaming new office buildings and mosques to a nondescript apartment complex. An American expatriate named Beetle Borden, who was hosting Jim and John, buzzed me up. Jim opened the door and gave me a big hug: "You made it, Leebo." He introduced me to Beetle, a friend of Jim's family who lawyered deals between American oil companies and the Iranian government. A few minutes later, a twenty-something man with wavy brown hair walked toward me. He wore jeans and a lumberjack shirt and he had a warm but mischievous smile.

THIRTY-THREE YEARS AFTER we first met, I received the following e-mail from John:

> Dear Lee-
> Great to hear from you. I was surprised to get the check because I don't remember the loan at all. I remember a lot about the trip but not that. I will give the money to my son, who is now the age we were in India, and ask him to spend it in some exotic place.

After all those years of inflating my debt's importance to him, it was strange for me to hear that John had absolutely no recollection of it. Still, I smiled at his choice of how to spend the money. With the help of his six hundred dollars, I had traveled to the shores of the Indian Ocean, as far away on earth as I could have been from where I grew up. At the age of twenty-two, I had moved among peoples and cultures I would read about in the news for the rest of my life. Now my six-hundred-dollar check would help John's son do the same thing.

I FLEW TO Denver in mid-June. John and I met at his office and drove to a bar on the outskirts of the city. At first I barely recognized him. He was slimmer and more professorial than I remembered, with thinning gray hair and a slight shuffle. But the more we talked and drank, the more I glimpsed the intrepid traveler who had steered Rosie through sandstorms and monsoons and over some of the world's most treacherous roads.

"Is it true that we had twenty-six flat tires in India alone?" I asked.

"Twenty-seven," he said.

"Remember the time you played chicken with the lorry and the lorry won and we started tumbling down the hill? I thought we were going to lose Rosie for good," I said.

"So did I," he said. "Then, out of nowhere, those villagers came, dozens of them, and wrapped ropes around Rosie and pulled us to safety."

"It was unbelievable," I said. "And how about the time we were traveling between Agra and Delhi and the dacoits, the bandits, jumped out of the trees."

"Yeah," he said. "They were after the bananas and jackfruit on top of the lorry in front of us. I had to haul ass to get us out of there."

The more we talked, the younger and more adventurous I felt. John was eager to pit his memories of the trip against mine.

We began with Beetle Borden's apartment in Tehran.

"Remember how Beetle told us to refer to the shah and his wife as George and Martha because he was sure Iranian intelligence was bugging his apartment?" I asked.

"Yeah," John said. "But instead of bugging Beetle and his buddies and hunting for Commies, the SAVAK should have been worrying about the ayatollahs, who took them totally by surprise."

"Yeah, I didn't see the ayatollahs coming, did you?" I asked.

"No," John said. "In fact, I don't remember hearing anything when we were there, do you?"

"Not a peep," I said. "No one talked politics in Iran. I guess they were too afraid."

"Yeah, it was eerie quiet."

After Tehran, we drove south through parched desert to Qom, the second holiest city of the Shia, and to the ancient urban centers of Kashan, Arak, and Isfahan in the foothills of the Zagros Mountains. Everywhere we went we visited the bazaars with their storied rugs, mosques with blue faience that cooled our eyes, and ruins of the great empires that had ruled Persia over the centuries. Outside the town of Kerman, at the northern edge of the Dasht-i-Lut desert in central Iran, I took photos of John standing next to Rosie in front of an old caravansary and an audience of scraggly goats. The next photo showed five women covered head to toe in black chadors. Their hands were raised to their mouths, giving the impression of deer caught in headlights.

"I'm glad their husbands didn't see you taking that picture," John said.

"I know."

In Tehran, John had found an old map of Alexander the Great's route through southeastern Persia. Our idea was to follow the route and write an article about it. So we pulled off the highway and began driving across the Dasht-i-Lut, searching for signs and landmarks of Alexander's trek back from India. The problem was there were no landmarks, only sand and more sand and 125-degree heat. After two days we found ourselves driving down a dried riverbed without food or water and on our last few gallons of petrol.

"How did you feel that night when we went to bed?" I asked John.

"Like we were going to die," he said. "Like it was going to be our last night on earth."

"And then a miracle happened. Remember?"

"Not exactly."

"When we woke up that morning, we heard the voices of children," I said. "It seemed like they were a hundred yards away. So we drove down the riverbed in their direction. We ended up driving for at least ten miles."

"And then we saw that group of nomads," John recalled. "What were they again?"

"Baluchi."

"Yes, Baluchi nomads. They looked like they had never seen Westerners before. An old woman served us tea and some food, some type of hot stew, and they drew us a map in the sand, pointed us southeast, and off we went. They saved our life."

"You've got a good memory," I said. I took out a photograph I had taken of the old woman, sitting stern and cross-legged in the sand. "Remember her?"

"I sure do," he said. "We finally got to a highway and found some petrol. Then we drove south to Bandar Abbas, on the Persian Gulf."

John was getting excited. As he talked, I pictured the city and water shimmering in the distance like an oasis. I also recalled something else.

"Do you remember what was so strange about Bandar Abbas?" I asked.

"All the Americans there, the oil workers," John said.

"Yup, there were a lot of Americans there. But I'm talking about the people we saw as we drove into the city, their eyes," I said.

"Yeah," John said. "They were blind. Women, children. It was out of a horror movie, the way they were walking around. They had some parasite, I think. It was sad—and strange."

"Then we went to a hotel for dinner," I said. "After starving in the desert, we wanted to treat ourselves to a nice, thick steak. Do you remember what happened?"

"The storm," he said.

"Yup, almost as soon as we got there, a hurricane hit. I went to the restroom. When I flushed the toilet, it was if a sewer exploded, all this excrement poured out. When I walked back into the restaurant, the water was up to my ankles. Then the lights went out. Most of the oilmen kept eating their steaks until they started sniffing and realized that something smelled pretty darn bad. Then everyone started going for the door. But the Iranians had locked us in."

"They were afraid we'd leave without paying our check," John said.

"They took us hostage," I said, "Just as the ayatollahs would a few years later."

*   *   *

BY THEN, JOHN and I were on a roll, reliving the highlights of our trip through Iran, Pakistan, and India. In the ancient mud city of Bam, in southern Iran, John got a terrible case of dysentery and couldn't eat or move for a week. The Dasht-i-Lut didn't kill him but it felt as though the dysentery would. It was so bad that we seriously considered driving him to the nearest airport and flying him back to the States. While John rested, Jim and I watched an Italian movie company make a spaghetti western in Bam's ancient ruins.

"I hated Bam," John said. "Did you know that a level 6.6 earthquake destroyed it a few years ago, killing twenty-five thousand people? Didn't we pick up a hitchhiker there?"

"Yeah, a British guy named Colin who smelled like patchouli oil," I said.

"When we got to the Pakistani border, the guards were all over him," he recalled. "I thought they were going to put him in jail."

"They just wanted to sell him drugs. That happened everywhere we went with Colin." I hadn't thought about our patchouli-scented hitchhiker in over thirty years.

From the border, we drove across Baluchistan with a Pakistani army convoy. At the time, there was a civil war going on and it would have been suicidal to cross the region alone.

"Do you remember the *tchai-khane*?" John asked.

"I do," I said.

We were both whispering. The *tchai-khane*, or teahouse, served as an overnight rest stop for lorry drivers traveling between Iran and India. Each of the lorry drivers had a young boy, and that night, more than a dozen of them slept on the floor cuddling with their companions, depriving us of the rest we needed to make the arduous drive to Quetta.

Today, Quetta is best known as a hideout for the Taliban and Al-Qaeda. But in 1976, foreigners traveling overland to Kabul or Kathmandu knew it for its charas, or hashish. Colin, a connoisseur of such things, gave us a guided tour of the city's opium and hashish

dens before he left us for good to join a group of reed-thin French
hippies who were smoking charas and coughing up blood.

From there, we traveled south to Shikarpur, in the Sindh region.
A man we met introduced us to Ghous Bux Khan Mahar, the tribal
leader in the region, who invited us to stay in his village. Each evening, the thirty-year-old khan would sit in his courtyard settling
marital and property disputes. After dinner, we would discuss politics with the khan, who was particularly intrigued by President Nix-
on's rise again to power, then fall. One night, I stupidly accepted the
khan's offer of an after-dinner drink made with water buffalo milk,
and fell deathly ill.

Just thinking about the khan made my stomach hurt—and John's
too. So, sitting outside the bar in Denver, we ordered another pitcher
of Coors and shared calmer memories, like the week we spent in
northern India harvesting sugarcane with a family of Sikhs, and the
afternoon we rode up to the maharaja of Jaipur's palace on an elephant. It was impossible to describe the fragrance of the great Mu-
ghal gardens of Pakistan and India or the perfect beauty of the Taj,
or the wretched look and taste of the fruit called durian, but we
tried.

TALKING AND SHARING stories with John brought back another
world, another time, another me, and shored up memories that had
begun to fade. And it also made me realize how lucky I had been to
travel after college with him and Jim. If I had been any less confused about my future, or any less naive, I would never have joined
up with them on the greatest adventure of my life.

We had traveled for different reasons. Jim wanted to gather experiences for a novel he was writing. John wanted to have one big adventure before going to law school and settling down. And I wanted
to get as far away as I could from the bitterness that divided my

family, the insularity that narrowed my thinking, and the fears that blurred my picture of the person I might be capable of becoming.

Seeing John helped me remember the day I finally got there—to the place on earth farthest away from Cleveland. I was standing on a beach in southern India, near Puri, watching the sun rise over the Bay of Bengal. I felt grungy, on edge, as if I hadn't bathed or slept in the months it had taken me to get there. But here I was, at the end and the beginning of the world, watching the sun grow bright and brighter in its rising, until all I could do was shield my eyes.

MY VISIT WITH John made me curious about Jim, who had been the architect of our plan to buy Rosie and travel to India. I had only gotten together with Jim a few times over the years, even though we lived less than three miles away from each other in Manhattan and had weekend homes less than two hours away from each other in Upstate New York.

When I wrote to him, I apologized for not keeping in better touch.

"No remiss on your part," he wrote back. "Keeping in touch is just part of the natural ebb and flow, Leebo."

After our Land Rover trip, Jim had rented an apartment in New York City's Little Italy, right across the street from the "social club" where mafia don John Gotti conducted business. To support his writing, he had worked as a waiter, bartender, book salesman, and software engineer. Then he started his own software company, which he sold. Now he was working four days a week as a software architect at a digital advertising firm in Manhattan. On Thursday nights he and his wife, Nancy, drove to Pine Hills, a small town at the foot of Belleayre Mountain in the Catskills, where Jim was creating what he called a "new form of live, electronic narrative" in a second-floor loft that he had rented above the Pine Hills Community Center.

I drove to Pine Hills to visit him. It was clear that the town had seen better days. Only a few stores were open and I was sorry to see that a restaurant that had served Indian food was shuttered.

When I called up to him from the street, Jim poked his head out the window and said, "Leebo. Great to see ya, buddy. Be right down." Jim was the only person in the world who still called me Leebo. He was also the only friend I had who wore his remaining gray hair in a ponytail that stretched down to his waist.

The center had been deeded to the community by the man who had invented the heat-resistant tiles used in the space shuttle. Its huge first floor, the size of an airplane hangar, held potluck dinners, computer and arts-and-crafts classes, a monthly variety show of local musicians and storytellers, and gatherings of the various groups that comprised the Pine Hill community, including Native Americans, the elderly, young people, and activists like Jim who were waging a grassroots campaign to keep big-city developers from turning Belleayre Mountain into a ski resort for the wealthy. Jim was proud of the role it played in providing services and hope to a region where nearly 25 percent of the people lived in poverty.

"What an absolutely wonderful place," I said. "You have a right to be proud of it."

"Thanks," Jim said. "Let's see Realto."

We climbed a rickety wooden stairway to the second-floor loft that served as Jim's studio. In a corner of the loft there was a large contraption that consisted of a video camera, a computer, and an LCD blue screen situated behind a small stage. Jim flicked a series of switches and the screen was filled with layers upon layers of computer-generated imagery and type.

"Now watch this," Jim said. When he stood on the stage, his figure was projected onto the screen, creating a truly strange and dynamic interaction between big Jim and little Jim, the narrator on stage and the character he was playing in the text.

"Realto," he said, and took a bow. "What do you think, Leebo?"

"Beyond cool," I said.

Jim seemed as happy as a kid who had just shown a friend the car he had cobbled together to win a soapbox derby competition. The big difference was that Jim had been working on this project for more than thirty years.

It began with a series of stories he wrote in college called "The Ferris Reels: The Autobiography of Cybernaut-01, Human Biocomputer." Jim got a fellowship to the University of Virginia to finish the book. But as soon as he got there, his apartment caught fire, burning up his only copy.

Most people would have taken such bad luck as a sign from the gods to move on, but Jim started writing his book again. It took him ten years to complete it. By then, he knew his mission in life: "I wanted to travel around the world as Cybernaut-01, Human Biocomputer, re-creating 'The Ferris Reels,' each night, before a live audience. That's what Dickens and Twain did. They traveled from city to city, giving serial performances of their books. But to do this for audiences in the twenty-first century, I needed to create a more visual and interactive storytelling experience."

For the past two years Jim had been engineering Realto to fit into two large suitcases. He was either a madman or a genius, and he knew it. "I know it's crazy, Leebo, but I'm going to keep tinkering with Realto until I can take 'Ferris Reels' to the people."

"When you do, I'll be sitting in the front row," I told him. "And I mean it."

ON THE DRIVE home, I realized that Jim and I hadn't said one word about the nine months we had spent traveling together. I had wanted to ask him how our trip had changed his life, but the question never came up. It was as if Realto had long supplanted Rosie in his life and I would only slow his momentum by asking him to look back. Jim was as much an adventurer at age fifty-five as he had been at twenty-two, and so was I, I had started to see. The days of driving through war zones and challenging our intestinal fortitude were over; those adventures were for younger men. But Jim was on a journey to make his Realto a reality and I was on one to complete the unfinished business of my life. Both of these journeys would test our character and courage, and they would be just as scary, challenging, and memorable as the times we steered clear of dacoits in India, got lost in the deserts of Iran, and stood on Puri beach, shielding our eyes from the blazing, merciless sun.

A FEW WEEKS after I visited John and Jim, I put my reclaimed identity as an enthusiastic, risk-taking adventurer to the test. Caroline had been away at sleepover camp for nearly a month and Elizabeth's plan was to take the boys hiking before we visited her. The unspoken expectation was that I would remain at the lodge, writing, while Elizabeth and the boys climbed Cascade Mountain and picnicked at its summit. But on the morning of the big hike, I told them to make room for Daddy.

"Sure, Pops," Noah said. "You're going to climb a mountain with us. A mountain, Pops. Sure, Pops. Sure."

I took Noah's taunting as a dare.

On the drive to the mountain, I stopped at an outfitter's store to buy myself a walking stick. Ben said that the ones with rubber tips on the bottom were "not cool," so I bought a plain wooden one for fifteen dollars. I felt well equipped. The stick gave me the confidence I would need to navigate the rocks and streams and keep from slipping.

Although the mountain was only two thousand feet high, the trail to the summit was over two miles long. I had forgotten how exhilarating hiking could be: how the forest cools you even as you sweat like a pack mule from your rock-to-rock exertion; how the sunlight streams through the leaves, illuminating a tiny tableau of moss and lichen on a fallen tree trunk; the pleasure that comes from simply being in a new and beautiful place.

The higher we climbed, the more I had to stop and catch my breath, which increased the distance between me and the boys. Elizabeth tried to stay within earshot, but at a certain point, I was simply too tired to keep going. As I headed back down, climbers on the way up would ask me about the view from the summit. "Unbelievable," I would say, even though I hadn't gotten anywhere near it.

I felt wonderful having gone as far up the mountain as I did. But I knew exactly what my two boys would say when they returned after reaching the summit.

Noah said, "You're a wimp, Pops."

"What do you mean?" I said.

"You only got a quarter of the way up."

"I made it halfway up," I said.

"A quarter, Dad, if that. And we're being generous," Ben said.

Whether I made it a half or a quarter of the way up didn't matter, because the story of the climb was far from over. While Ben and Noah were trudging to the summit, I was sitting in our minivan reflecting on the days when I drove high into the foothills of the Himalayas, within sight of Everest and K-2, with Jim and John. What, I wondered, was the thread that connected those days with this one?

When I paid John back for the six hundred dollars he loaned me, I did it to lessen the amount of guilt I was carrying around. But our reunion ended up enriching me in a dozen other ways. It gave me a chance to remember forgotten pleasures, such as the taste of jackfruit, the view from Dal Lake on a misty morning, and the sound of a muezzin calling his village to midday prayer. It helped me to reexperience the part of myself that used to welcome each new day as an adventure. And it opened my eyes to the opportunity every parent has to create adventures with their own children. Perhaps that was the thread.

When I returned to New York, I told Noah that if he woke me up by six thirty the next morning, I would take him to the diner for breakfast before he went to school.

He woke me up at five thirty. On our way to the diner, we stopped to watch as the early-morning trucks dispatched fresh fruits and vegetables to the Korean grocery stores. We passed joggers and dog walkers and men and women in suits hurrying to the subway.

Once we were there, Noah ordered the biggest breakfast on the menu—lumberjack pancakes, with sides of ham, sausage, and bacon—and a chocolate milkshake. He told me how much he hated the Yankees and loved our dogs and his math teacher. By the time we left, the diner was filled with the happy glow of sunrise. And we felt like "two drifters, off to see the world, there's such a lot of world to see," as Johnny Mercer had put it.

It's a memory we'll both cherish, because we created it together.

So whether I got a quarter of the way up or halfway up doesn't matter. The story of our climb up Cascade Mountain won't be finished until next year, when I make it to the top.

CHAPTER FOUR

I've Been Thinking of You
Since the Planes Struck

Reaching Out to a Distant Friend

EVER SINCE 9/11, I had been worried about the safety of a Pakistani friend of mine who disappeared from my life nearly thirty years ago. I was nostalgic about the times we had spent together, and curious and concerned about where life might have taken him in these newly violent times.

When I was in my midtwenties, I supported myself by working as a bartender at the Mad Greek, a restaurant in suburban Cleveland that was owned by an Indian immigrant and his feisty Greek-American wife.

It was a fun place to work, full of beautiful young waitresses who aspired to be actresses—and a thirty-year-old Pakistani grad student who sported a handlebar mustache and giggled like a thirteen-year-old schoolboy. His name was Akmal and he giggled because he couldn't believe that Allah had given him the great good fortune of waiting tables in the midst of so many beautiful women.

Akmal and I didn't just work together; we were roommates. We shared a house with a recently divorced, marathon-running labor-and-delivery nurse named Bruce. All three of us were between lives. Bruce was studying to become a podiatrist, Akmal was preparing to return to Pakistan and begin a psychotherapy practice, and I was back in Cleveland after traveling abroad. Besides bartending, I was writing about photography for a local arts magazine and trying to get my first poems published. In my spare time, I worried about what I would do for the rest of my life.

Most of my poems had to do with Elsie, the actress/waitress who was my girlfriend and muse. We would give readings of my poetry at libraries, coffee shops, and on the radio. As a kid, even as a college student, I had been terrified of speaking in front of other people. But for some reason, pledging my love to Elsie in front of a room filled with strangers was exhilarating.

I broke up with Elsie more than I liked to admit—at least once a month—but there were times when I would do anything to be around her. So when Akmal ran out of options for getting a green card, I urged him to marry Elsie, who was game to help. Theirs wasn't a real marriage, but Elsie needed to stay at our house to fend off any inquiries the immigration agency might have into the legitimacy of their relationship. It served my purpose well. I got to sleep with my muse without worrying that she might be sleeping elsewhere.

Before Akmal went back to Pakistan in the winter of 1981, he and Elsie got divorced. Elsie and I also broke up—this time for good. She fell in love with a waiter who was studying to be an opera singer. And I began hanging out with photographers, filmmakers, lawyers, psychologists, writers, college professors, and even an entrepreneur or two to see which of their professions might suit me. I liked being around people who were passionate about their careers, and I was still at that age when you think you can do and become anything. Eventually I decided to move to New York and become a journalist. It seemed like a good way to keep learning, writing, and exploring the world. If that didn't work out, I could always become something else.

I WAS STILL living in Cleveland when I received the only letter Akmal wrote me after he returned to Pakistan. It was dated March 15, 1982.

Dear Lee,

Asalamu Alaichum

You must be wondering whether I am dead or alive? My dear friend, this transition of mine has not been an easy one. In some ways I have been alive, but mourning the death of the parts of me that had flourished and come to existence due to that wonderful country of yours, which has so many beautiful, warm and honest souls like you. I was not able to write to you earlier because every time I tried to do it, the feelings and emotions would overwhelm me.

Since he had been back in Lahore, Akmal had been working day and night to build his practice and his hard work was beginning to pay off:

I launched a fairly organized campaign to get ads in the newspaper, printed 600 announcement cards and mailed them to all of the psychiatrists and most of the senior doctors and professors at Lahore's medical colleges. In my private practice I have 14 patients. So now I feel a bit more secure in my profession, and I am sure the worst months are over, and that things are going to get better every day.

As anyone who knew my friend would have expected, he was ready to launch phase two of his plan. He had purchased a used VW Beetle. And he was applying for a government loan that would enable him to build the house he had designed with an architect friend. After he built the house, his goal was to fill it with a family. But first he would need a wife. A real wife. He reported that not much had happened as far as girls were concerned. "I haven't had the energy. But now I am feeling pretty horny."

The letter was vintage Akmal. Within weeks of returning to

Pakistan, he had established the Lahore Institute of Psychotherapy. His tagline—"Helping you fight the fears in your life"—reflected the seriousness with which he would market himself. If he stayed on plan, he was certain he would succeed. At the end of the letter, he invited me to be "generous and frequent" in writing him and to give his "Comesta" (short for "como esta usted," "how are you" in Spanish) to everyone he knew, including Elsie.

But I had been neither generous nor frequent in writing to my friend. In fact, in the twenty-six years since I last heard from him, I had not written him at all. After I moved to New York and got my graduate degree in journalism, I quickly became a slave to the weekly deadlines that punctuated the next two decades of my career. One thing led to another and I pretty much forgot about Akmal until that bright and surreal September morning when I heard rumors that something terrible had just happened in lower Manhattan. I was on a crosstown bus en route to a doctor's appointment. The woman next to me got a call on her cell phone from her father in Israel who had just seen on CNN that a plane had crashed into the World Trade Center, only three miles away from us. By the time I got to the doctor's, people were wandering the streets of Manhattan in panic and disbelief: A second plane had struck.

As the days and weeks went on, I kept thinking about Akmal. It was impossible to imagine my gentle, earnest, hardworking friend thriving in a culture that had somehow encouraged fanatics to crash planes into skyscrapers, ending the lives of so many innocent people. I thought about the years we roomed together in Cleveland. It seemed a world and lifetime away, and it was. Then there had been time to make of it what you would, time for just hanging out in the park or on the stoop in the evening, flirting with girls and chatting with passing neighbors. There had been time for friends and friendship.

We all had lived a life of minimal commitment and endless possibilities. Everyone I knew—Bruce, Elsie, even Abe, our photogra-

pher friend—was in a state of becoming. After hours at the Mad
Greek, we'd drink and dance and dream. We carried ourselves with
a bit of swagger, but really we were broke and living hand to mouth.
If one of us needed a doctor or some legal advice, a month's rent or a
new muffler, we'd pool our resources and find a way to help. If one
of us broke up with our boyfriend or girlfriend, the rest of us would
offer a couch and an ear. Because we had no one else, we were there
for each other. You might not want to live that way forever, but looking back, it was one of the most romantic periods of my life.

That era ended as soon as I moved to New York. I was about to
turn twenty-nine. At that age, it didn't seem as cool to spend as much
time dancing and daydreaming. It was time to carve out a career
path and get serious about being an adult. This meant narrowing
possibilities and making some choices. Because I had little prepara-
tion for that task, I felt a need to protect myself from anything that
might distract me. As the biblical saying goes, it was time to "put away
childish things." Perhaps I took the instruction too literally. Akmal
wasn't the only friendship that suffered as a result.

The events of 9/11 changed that. I was genuinely concerned about
the safety of my old friend, who was living in the region that became
ground zero in the clash between Islam and the West. As a Western-
educated professional, Akmal could find his career and family at risk
if there was a war or revolution in his country. But I was also being
pulled in Akmal's direction for a reason that had nothing to do with
9/11: Akmal was one of my last true links to the period of my life
when I was "still a child, playing with childish things." I didn't want
to lose one of my best connections to the time in my life when I had
minimal responsibilities, wrote poetry, and felt that I could be anything I dreamt of being. And on top of it all, when I allowed myself
to really think about it, I simply missed my old friend.

I would think of Akmal a lot over the next few years. And then
the oddest thing happened. Just as I was beginning to formulate
my project of attending to my unfinished business, a project in

which reconnecting with Akmal would be a high priority, my youngest son, Noah, brought me the phone and said that someone wanted to speak with me.

"Who is it?" I asked.

"Someone with a funny voice," he said.

"Is it a man or a woman?"

"A man."

"What does he want?"

"To talk to you. He has a funny voice."

"Like how funny?" I asked.

"Like Apu in *The Simpsons*."

"Like Apu?" I said, thinking that it might be a telemarketer calling from India.

I took the phone and said hello, fully expecting to end the caller's pitch before he began. But the man with the Apu voice had no product to pitch. Instead, he said, "Comesta, Lee?"

"Akmal?" I asked. I was in total, gleeful shock. It was as if I had spoken with my friend yesterday.

"Yes, Lee. It is Akmal. Comesta, old buddy?"

"I'm great," I said. "But how about you? This is so crazy. I was just thinking about how I wanted to find you."

"And I've been trying to find you for days, amigo. I had no idea where you were. Finally, I located Abe and he gave me your number. I am calling from Mississauga."

"Missi-what?

"Mississauga. It's near Toronto. I intend to move here with my family."

"Your family? You have a family? You need to tell me everything."

He didn't tell me everything, but he did tell me enough to ease my mind and whet my appetite for more. Since I had last seen him, Akmal had built a successful private practice in Lahore and headed a school for autistic children. Not long after he wrote me, his parents arranged for his marriage to a woman named Nausheen who worked as a pathologist; they had had three children, two girls and one boy, and one of their daughters had just been awarded a Fulbright scholarship to Cornell University, about three hours away from me in Ithaca, New York.

Akmal decided to move his family to Canada so that he could be closer to his daughter and give his fifteen-year-old son the type of education and advantages that America had given him. He was in Mississauga interviewing for jobs and looking for an apartment; his goal was to move to Mississauga with his family in a year.

"When will I see you?" I asked him.

"I leave tomorrow. I'll be back in Canada over the summer. Can you visit me in Lahore?"

"I'd love to," I said. "But I'll need to speak with Elizabeth. She'll be nervous about my traveling there."

Later that day I received an e-mail from Akmal.

Dear Lee,
Finding out where you are, then getting hold of your phone number, was not easy. Then I heard your voice again. It was so energizing and nourishing, I still feel a high. I think it will be very healing for me to have this long overdue meeting with you, because it will give me a chance to attend to my own unfinished business. Tell me what Elizabeth says. Salaam Aleichum.

It seemed that Akmal had needed me as much as I needed him and for a similar reason: to help him complete a piece of *his* unfinished business. I had absolutely no idea what it was, but I was anxious to find out. I told Elizabeth that I wanted to visit Akmal and his wife in Pakistan.

Elizabeth said, "You are not going."

"Why?" I asked.

"I'll give you three reasons," she said. "Benjamin, Caroline, and Noah."

"You're being ridiculous," I said. "It's not like I haven't been there before."

"That was over thirty years ago," she said. "Things are different now."

"Not as different as you think," I countered.

"They are," she said. "You've got three children now—and me."

We agreed to suspend our debate until my trip to Pakistan was closer to becoming a reality. But it never got that far. Right before Thanksgiving, Akmal called with some surprising news. "Comesta, Lee? I'm in Mississauga."

"What are you doing there?" I asked.

"I got a job here. I'm working as a counselor and therapist at a social services agency. It's a good job, so I decided to move here earlier than I had expected. I'll bring Nausheen and the kids over in July, after the school year is over."

"When can I see you?" I asked.

"How about next weekend?"

AKMAL PICKED ME up at the Toronto International Airport. But it would be at least half an hour before I would feel relaxed talking with him. Getting out of the parking lot and onto the highway and into the proper traffic lane, then off at the right exit challenged every bit of his attention, as well as my own. I would have been just as nervous had I been the one navigating a new city. So I made halfhearted small talk and didn't feel offended when Akmal didn't answer me.

It wasn't until he'd parked the car and made his way through the concrete garage to the elevator that Akmal began to loosen up and focus on the fact that he was welcoming an old friend to his new life. We took the elevator up to the twenty-sixth floor. Then he took out his key and opened the door to his new home.

"Well, here we are, Lee. It is nice to see you again," he said. "Please make yourself comfortable while I turn down the heat and get us a glass of water."

What struck me most about Akmal's apartment, beyond the fact that it rose twenty-six stories above Square One Shopping Center, one of the largest malls in North America, and had a bird's-eye view of the five highways that led from Toronto to the rest of Canada, was its size: There was a bedroom, bathroom, and living room/kitchen area, all nicely appointed, but way too small for the family of three who would be joining him in July.

From photographs I knew that Akmal and his family occupied a spacious home in Lahore and had four servants—a cook, a chauffeur, a laundress, and a maid. In a country where the per capita income was $926, Akmal and his wife Nausheen were well off. Here he and Nausheen would need to do their own shopping, cooking, and laundry and wait in line for the bathroom until their children were finished using it. Was Akmal concerned about this sudden drop in his quality of life?

"For many years I felt that I was stagnating in Pakistan, that I wasn't challenging myself or learning anything new," he said. "To pursue my new dream will require sacrifice, my friend, but I have much to gain."

Akmal's dream was to live half the year in Canada, serving that country's growing population of immigrants from his part of the world. "My work at the clinic will help me learn the ropes and make contacts," he said. "Most of my sixty-year-old colleagues in Pakistan are preparing to retire. I am at the beginning of a new adventure."

That night I accompanied Akmal to his office Christmas party. To most people, or at least to me, an office holiday party is a command performance you endure rather than enjoy. You sip a drink, make small talk, and wait for the boss to leave before you either let down your hair or head for the coat-check room.

If you had seen Akmal pick up his name card and pin it to the lapel of his sport coat, then adjust it so it would be easy for everyone to read; if you had seen him survey the room and greet every new person as if he or she were the most important person in the world, his smile widening beneath his white handlebar mustache, his eyes sparkling beneath his distinguished white hair; if you had heard him say, "Hello, my name is Akmal, I have just begun working at the clinic, it is a pleasure to meet you and to be your colleague," you would have thought, "What a genuinely sweet guy," which would have been true. But even truer, you would have been witnessing the only person in that packed ballroom who considered this party an important milestone in both his personal and professional growth.

Later that evening Akmal's old school chum, Shahid, joined us for a cup of tea. Shahid had been living in Mississauga since he graduated law school. He had three grown children and worked in the Ministry of Government and Consumer Services as a workplace discrimination adviser. Shahid was a jovial fellow, full of schemes to get rich and famous and change the world. But, when push came to shove, Shahid was a bureaucrat by both temperament and pay grade—and in this sense, he was Akmal's polar opposite.

"It's a very good idea, Lee, this project you have undertaken," Shahid said. "We all have unfinished business—things we should have done but didn't. And we need to make an accounting of these things before we die, so that our souls can rest."

Akmal had a different take on what I was doing. "It's not about resting in peace," he said. "It's about moving forward. It's about optimizing your human potential."

"How do you mean?" Shahid asked.

Akmal took a sip of his tea. "To get things done, you need to have a certain amount of psychological energy," he said. "Say you have ten kilograms of that energy available to you in a day. The amount is fixed. By not resolving your unfinished business, you deplete that energy."

As an example, Akmal asked us to consider what happens when we leave home without telling our wives why we are angry at them.

"By keeping your anger in, you expend half a kilogram of your daily energy. Another half is lost when your boss chews you out and you do not defend yourself. When you feel like crying but do not, you lose another half. And so on. Each time you deflect or block something, you pay a price for it, which is subtracted from the total energy you have available to you. Is my explanation clear, Shahid?"

"Clear as a bell," he laughed. "My wife was expecting me home hours ago. My psychological energy, as you call it, is about the same as my chances of getting laid tonight: zero."

"Unless you bring her a bouquet of red and yellow roses and tell her how much you love her," Akmal said.

"How well do you know my wife, my friend?" Shahid asked playfully.

"Do you really want to know?" Akmal giggled.

"What you said makes a lot of sense to me," I said to Akmal, stifling my own giggle.

"My job as a therapist is to lessen the amount of unfinished business that is sapping my clients' energy," Akmal said. "If I can help them save that energy, they will be able to reinvest it in the present and lead fuller lives."

"That's what I'm trying to do," I said. "I'm trying to lessen my load of bad karma so that I can lead a fuller, truer life."

"I know," he said.

I knew he knew. He knew because his whole career had been devoted to knowing such things. And he knew because he had known the me who had loved walking the streets of Cleveland and Lahore with my camera, taking photographs of whatever touched my fancy, and he had known the me who had considered becoming everything from a massage therapist to a lawyer, and he had known the me who had given him my girlfriend so that he could get a green card. Akmal had known a me that I wanted to find and reclaim again.

*   *   *

ON SATURDAY MORNING, we drove to one of the many nondescript office buildings lining the highways on the outskirts of Mississauga. The parking lot was empty—and so was the lobby, save for a Pakistani janitor who was vacuuming the carpeting and stairway.

Akmal and I took the elevator to the second floor, where Akmal shared office space with another therapist—and where he was scheduled, at eleven A.M., to have a consultation with his first private client. I could tell that Akmal was excited: In his gray slacks, blue blazer, and red tie, he was poised to make a good first impression. I didn't want to get in his way. So fifteen minutes before his scheduled appointment, I disappeared with a magazine into an adjacent office.

The next thing I knew, Akmal was shaking me. "Wake up, Lee. You fell asleep." I was lying on the couch, the magazine open on my chest.

"Was I snoring?" I asked.

"Loudly," he said.

"How did your session go?" I asked.

"It didn't," he said. "My client never showed."

"Did he call?"

"No," Akmal said. "It is not uncommon for a client to get cold feet at the last minute."

Knowing how much this first meeting meant to him, I felt terrible for Akmal. "Would you like to wait a few more minutes for him?" I asked.

"Thank you, Lee, but it will not be necessary," he said. "You must be very hungry after your nap."

"Some things never change," I laughed.

"Then let us go for lunch," he said.

As we walked down the hall, we saw the Pakistani custodian standing in a dark corner of the hallway, along with two other janitors who looked Pakistani. They had taken off their shoes and placed prayer rugs on the floor. Then, as the Koran dictated, they began praying toward the east, in the direction of Mecca. I had seen Muslims pray in a similar fashion all over the world. Standing erect, they touched their thumbs to their earlobes and said in unison, "Allahu akbar!" ("God is great!"). Then they bowed from their hips and placed their hands on their knees, saying in Arabic, "I extol the perfection of my Lord the Great." Then they stood upright again and repeated "Allahu akbar!"

"Do you ever pray like that?" I asked Akmal as we exited the lobby. I couldn't remember him ever praying or attending a mosque when we lived together, but maybe things had changed since he met and married Nausheen.

"I only pray like that during the month of Ramadan," he said. "I am Muslim but not observant. When I was growing up, my father prayed five times daily. Nausheen and I do not."

I wondered if the fact that he had chosen to have an arranged marriage meant that he would want his children to have arranged marriages—and to lead a more conventional life than the one he had led before he got married. I certainly hoped that my own children would lead lives that led them to marry before I did, at age forty-three; otherwise, I might never have the pleasure of being a grandfather until I was over eighty, a thought that saddened me.

"My kids can do as they please," he said.

"Remember my parents? How much they worried about my future?" I asked.

"I do," he said. "They hated the fact that you had become a bartender and wanted to write. They thought that you, their eldest, with the Ivy League education, would never get a job with health insurance. They didn't like Elsie much either, because she wasn't Jewish and worked as a waitress. I remember how much that bothered you."

"It did," I said. "It drove me nuts. Your parents, on the other hand, must have been overjoyed that you returned to Pakistan and married a Muslim."

"Of course they were," he said. "But there was never any question about that. I was their only child. It was my duty to take care of them until they died. And it was my duty to marry a nice Muslim girl."

"Does Nausheen know about Elsie?" I asked.

I could still remember the day Akmal and Elsie got married. The ceremony took place in the office of the justice of the peace. Akmal and I wore the only sport coats we owned. Elsie wore a white granny dress. I was the best man, flower girl, and photographer. After the justice of the peace administered the oath, there was a good deal of winking and hugging but no ring or kiss. Then we were out the door. That night we had a small party at the house, with toasts and dancing, before Elsie and I went off to bed.

Had Akmal kept Elsie a secret from Nausheen?

"I told her about Elsie before we got married," Akmal said. "She was fine with it. Many of her friends had been forced to do the same thing in order to finish their education or get a green card."

THE RESTAURANT HE had chosen, an all-you-can-eat buffet, was full of harried parents and their kids. They piled pizza, sushi, pudding, steamed vegetables, dumplings, barbecued chicken, brownies, and pork spare ribs on their plates, and when they were done, they went back for more, as did we. We sat at a table in the back, talking about our time together in Cleveland.

After our second plateful of steamed dumplings, Akmal said, "Those years in Canada and Cleveland changed my life, my friend."

"What do you mean?" I asked.

"Before coming here," he said, "I would give only 40 percent of myself to whatever I did. Here I learned to give 100 percent of myself. I began to take charge of my life and commit myself more fully to my work and my relationships, to everything."

The waitress brought over the pot of tea that we had ordered. Akmal thanked her and poured each of us a cup.

"Cheers," he said.

"Cheers."

"If I had remained in Pakistan during my twenties and thirties and not come to America, I would have never become even a small fraction of the person I was capable of becoming. I was that lazy and casual about things."

From the years we lived together, it was hard for me to picture Akmal as being lazy about anything. In addition to going to graduate school and waiting tables, he volunteered twice a week as an intake worker at Cleveland's free clinic and counseled patients at the slightly more upscale Institute of Rational-Emotive Therapy. His patients at the clinic struggled with drug abuse, alcoholism, unemployment, and marital strife, problems he had never encountered in his own life. The experience transformed him.

"Previously, in school and college, I wasn't very courageous," he said. "But in Cleveland I began to take risks and extend my boundaries. I learned to make choices and to take responsibility for them. Even the Mad Greek was a growth experience for me."

"How do you mean?" I asked.

"When I had to serve dishes and wipe tables and peel potatoes, I became connected to something that had been missing in my life. Back home there was a lot of emphasis on studying and getting a job with your brain. But anything having to do with manual labor, with using your hands, was looked down upon. At the Mad Greek, I felt whole."

One thing I had always wondered was whether Akmal had experienced much prejudice in America. Did he get fewer tips at the restaurant than he thought he deserved because he had dark skin and a heavy accent? Did anyone ever accuse him of being a terrorist?

"No, no," he said. "When I first got to Canada, hooligans called me 'Paki' once or twice. But it was never more than that."

I had also wondered if being Pakistani had inhibited his love life. Akmal always seemed to have girls who were friends, but he seldom had a girlfriend, and when he did, the relationship seemed to last only a few weeks. "Were there women who wouldn't go out with you because you were Pakistani?"

"No," he said. "The only negatives were the restraints I placed upon myself."

"What do you mean?" I asked.

He paused, it seemed forever, before he answered. "In spite of my having several girlfriends—and these were really nice, beautiful relationships—I would only let myself emotionally be intimate or involved to a certain extent, and then I'd put a stop to the relationship."

"Why do you think you did that?" I asked.

"Because I was afraid of myself," he said. "I was afraid of becoming involved to an extent that I would get married here and never go back to Pakistan. That was my way of . . ." Akmal did not complete the sentence. Instead, he started crying. He cried for so long and so hard that people throughout the restaurant looked over at us, and a waitress came by to see if we were okay.

"Thank you. I am fine," he told her.

After he wiped his tears and blew his nose with his hankie, he continued. "There were many relationships I wanted to explore, and I didn't give any of them a chance."

"Why?" I asked.

"How could I get involved with a woman in Canada or the States when I knew that I would be returning to Pakistan to take care of my aging parents?" he said. "It would have been unfair to the woman and to me." Then he finished the sentence he had started before he began sobbing. "It was my way of protecting myself," he said. "It was my way of staying my parents' good child."

I had never been aware of how much Akmal had built his entire life around his obligation to his parents—and how it had held him back and caused him pain. At a time when he had committed himself to "optimizing" his full potential as a human being, at a time when he was discovering parts of himself that he hadn't previously known, at a time when he was pushing ahead on every single emotional and physical cylinder, he had put on the brakes and limited his ability to love. And now, by returning to Canada and the United States, he was ready to acknowledge the pain and move beyond it.

We had come to this shared moment with the same purpose in mind: to reconcile our old selves with our new ones. And to weave both the past and each other into the separate stories of our lives.

To understand my own story, I craved Akmal's perspective on our life together in Cleveland and on me: "What do you remember most?" I asked.

"About you?" he said. "Well, it was exciting for me to have a roommate who was familiar with my part of the world. I liked your energy and spirit of adventure and you were interested in learning about other people and cultures. And you were such a good talker. You would engage people by teasing them, then backing off. I always wanted some of that to rub off on me, but it didn't. You attracted a lot of people."

I had forgotten that part of myself. When I met Akmal, I had just come back from India and was full of stories. Once I became a family man and magazine editor and started traveling mainly on business, I had fewer stories to tell and less need to impress people with my adventures. I missed that part of me. But perhaps it was the price I paid for moving on, for becoming an adult. Perhaps we all pay a price for growing up.

"We shared a study," Akmal said. "It was very inspiring for me to see you working on your typewriter."

As I remembered it, I spent most of my time staring out the window at the community garden. When Akmal and I moved into the house, the garden was barren. By the time we left, it was bustling with ponytailed farmers of both genders who tilled the soil with rakes and hand hoes and harvested tomatoes, cucumbers, and lettuce.

Our next-door neighbor was a dour malcontent who avoided eye contact as he shuffled down the street toward his job as a file clerk. He later became famous as the creator of the *American Splendor* comic books.

Sometimes the file clerk would cross paths with our buddy Abe, who would be walking as quickly as he could toward our house. Abe's nearby photography studio didn't have a bathroom, so he would occupy ours for hours at a time. Abe's sense of toilet entitlement was so urgent and predictable that I never challenged it. Instead, I would hurry to the coffee shop down the street and join the other caffeine- and nicotine-starved wretches who debated art and politics as they waited for a stall.

At times I was really hard on myself. Because I had trouble committing to my writing and to Elsie, I wondered if there was something terribly wrong with me. My worst fear was that I'd end up being a coffeehouse hippie or middle-aged bartender who talked endlessly about writing the great American novel but never wrote a word.

"When I left, Lee, you were toying with the idea of whether to be a journalist, a lawyer, a writer, or go into film," Akmal said. "You were ad hoc in your work and sporadic in your relationships.

"Finding out what you've done since is a happy experience for me, because you have achieved a lot. And that's something you could only have done through hard work and commitment."

Now I was the one who felt like sobbing. In the past twenty years, I had never stopped working or thinking about work long enough to appreciate what I had done. At age fifty-five, I still felt like a small boy hungering for a father's praise. Akmal gave me a huge dollop of it by recognizing that I had achieved what I had through the focus and commitment I had so clearly lacked in my twenties. His pride in me made me proud of myself and left me tongue-tied.

"Forgive me," I finally said. "I've never been good at patting myself on the back."

"I know," Akmal said. "But when you deserve it, Lee, you need to tell yourself, 'Job well done.' And don't forget to celebrate the small breakthroughs. It's a lesson I learned from the children I teach. When an autistic child touches another child or uses three words in a sentence, it can be as huge an achievement as landing on the moon."

BECAUSE AKMAL COULD see it in me, and I could see it in him, I could finally grasp a simple truth: We were who we are; we are who we were, only more so.

I had tended to see my twenties as either the golden age of endless possibilities or the lost decade when I couldn't get my act together. In fact, it was both. It was one of the most important stages in my life, the one that marked my passage from adolescence into adulthood. There was no reason to wax overly nostalgic or beat myself up over that period in my life, or perhaps any period. The women I went out with—and the poems I wrote to Elsie—were prelude to the genuinely committed relationship I would one day have with Elizabeth and the offspring we would produce. The sentences and paragraphs on the crunched-up pieces of paper I threw in the wastebasket were the seeds of the ideas that would guide my professional career. Everything in one's life—every person and experience—is part of everything else.

WHEN I BEGAN this journey, I was worried about Akmal's safety. I was afraid that he and his family were victims of the violence and chaos engulfing their part of the world. Luckily they were not. And instead of a rescue operation, our journey together became an exploration of what happens in two distinct periods of a man's life. In a youth of endless possibility, a man has the energy and moxie to pursue any woman or career and open any door. Decades later, most of those doors are closed. But the door you have chosen may open into the place you really belong.

As Akmal and I drove off into our adulthood, we were afraid of the temptations still visible in the rearview mirror. Would Akmal be lured back to the West and away from his obligation to his parents? Would his longing for old friends inhibit his devotion to his new life with Nausheen? I had similar fears. Would my memory of Elsie and my fellow dreamers in Cleveland prevent me from committing myself to a family and career?

In moving ahead, Akmal and I left our friendship behind. Then we both felt the urge to reconnect. In the end, we discovered for ourselves an ancient truth: There is a season for everything. There is a season to crawl and walk in the shadow of our parents, a season to stretch our legs and explore every conceivable path, a season to choose one single path that takes us deeper into the forest, and a season to build a home in the clearing and fill it with friends and children.

There is a season for taking care of our unfinished business, for tying up our loose ends. And there is a season for sitting around the fire with an old friend, weaving all that we've learned and experienced into a shared story.

THAT NIGHT AKMAL cooked me a traditional Pakistani meal of chicken biryani, salad, chapati, cucumber-mint raita, and gulab jamun for dessert. As I sat in the living room, on the couch bed, watching a hockey game on TV, the odors of an earlier era in my life filled the room: ginger, bay leaves, and cardamom to flavor the basmati rice, ghee dabbed on durum to soften the chapati, a pungent dash of curry.

When we lived together in Cleveland, Akmal cooked meals like the one we were about to eat whenever one of our Indian or Pakistani friends embarked on a journey. It could be an actual journey—for example, when P. K. went back to India to see his ailing father. Or it could be a journey of the heart—for example, when Loki decided to reconcile with Nikki, his Greek wife, or when our friend Muz found a girlfriend. That night's meal would mark two journeys—Akmal's to Canada and mine to visit him—and the renewal of our friendship. But it would also mark the two new chapters in our lives. Akmal opened up a bottle of red wine. We toasted everything good in our lives, including our wives and kids. Then we dug in. We used our right hands (never our left) to scoop up the rice and chicken with pieces of chapati. We soothed our hot tongues with cool and flavorful raita. We scraped the still-simmering chicken to the bone. Then we gobbled down the supersweet dough balls called gulab jamun, and threw caution to the wind.

"Comesta, amigo?"

"Better, my friend. And very full."

"Salaam Aleichem."

"Aleichem Salaam."

CHAPTER FIVE

Forgive Me the Harm
I Wished on You

Letting Go of a Grudge

FOR ALL THREE years of high school, Trip was my nemesis. He did everything he could to tarnish my glory and stab me in the back. It began when we played varsity football our sophomore year. Whenever I would run through the left side of the line in practice, Trip would knock me on my ass.

He was able to do this because the offensive guard on my team would tip Trip off whenever I was headed his way. On one such play, Trip hit me with such explosive and unchallenged force that my two front teeth tore through my lip and I was rushed to the hospital. One of those teeth broke in half and was capped with a fake tooth that was so yellow and oversized that I still keep my lips clamped together when I smile.

In his multiyear campaign to unravel me, Trip mobilized his friends to vote me off the student council and deprive me of the only leadership role in high school I really wanted. It was Trip, not me, who became captain of the baseball team, even though I had earned more varsity letters and pitched for the best summer sandlot team in the city. I thought of Trip as my personal Hitler. He made me feel overly sensitive and intellectual as well as conspicuously, vulnerably Jewish.

He didn't achieve this by painting swastikas on my locker or by sending me anonymous notes accusing me of being a Christ killer. He did it by grinning—no, sneering—at me. Trip's sneer pushed all of my buttons. It told me, "You are not what you pretend to be,

Kravitz. You are an intellectual suck-up, a fumbler of footballs, a baseball has-been, a Jew."

I will always remember the way he looked at me and my high school girlfriend, Joyce, as we were slow dancing at my senior prom. Trip maneuvered his date closer to us, held her tight, then tighter, then measured Joyce head to toe with his eyes. His grin seemed to say, "Look over here, Kravitz. Take a look at my squeeze. If you think you'll ever get a chance with a girl like her, dream on."

Trip was a genius at exploiting my weaknesses and making me feel two inches tall. In the four decades I didn't see or talk with him, he kept tormenting me—in my dreams. It was as if he had burrowed a hole in my psyche and taken up residence there, where his goal was to eviscerate me. I associated only bad things with Trip.

In the spring of 2007, I heard that Trip was dead. A friend told me that the Texas state police had found him lying in a ditch with two empty bottles of vodka at his side.

For years I had wished the worst for him—a tooth for my tooth, and more. But now that Trip had died a more horrific death than I could imagine for him, I felt only sadness and guilt. I couldn't put my finger on it, but my business with Trip was far from finished. So on one of my visits to Cleveland to see Fern, I called up Trip's best friend from high school and arranged to meet him for a drink.

I MET FRANK at a restaurant in Chagrin Falls, a fashionable Cleveland suburb. It was hard to couple this affable, kindhearted family man with the dissolute drinker Trip had become. But they had roomed together during college and stayed friends until Trip died.

"Did he have a drinking problem in college?" I asked.

"No more than anyone else," Frank said. "We all got tanked. I did. Trip did. We all did."

I described how Trip had singled me out for torment in high

school because I was different. I offered, as my prime example, the scrimmage in which he broke my tooth.

"I must have heard that story thirty times," Frank said. "Trip loved that story."

"So why did he do it? Why did he single me out?"

"He didn't," Frank said. "When he told that story, I don't remember Trip ever mentioning your name. What he would describe was his system: how Dave, at offensive guard, would drop into his stance, then signal with his fingers where the running backs were headed. A three-finger stance meant the hole between the tackle and end; two fingers meant the hole between tackle and guard; one finger signaled the hole between guard and center. By the time the running back got there, the chances of getting by Trip were slim. It wasn't about you or anyone else. It was about Trip wanting to make the first team.

"And I don't think that Trip got pleasure from knocking your tooth out," Frank added. "I take that back. Trip definitely got a kick out of other people's misery, mine as much as anyone else's. But it could have been anyone's tooth and he would have enjoyed it. The fact that it was your tooth meant nothing to Trip. And I think you're wrong in thinking that he was anti-Semitic. I never saw any evidence of that. Really."

My desire to make amends had been predicated on my certainty that Trip had hated and tormented me more than anyone else and that my feelings of revenge were based on perceptions that were real. Now I was learning that I wasn't special to him at all.

"I have to say that I don't get why you're so obsessed with Trip," Frank said. "He led such a sad life."

Frank described Trip's failed attempts at rehab: how he went from Hazelden, where celebrities dry out, to living among winos at a single-room occupancy hotel in one of the worst sections of Cleveland. From time to time, he would ask Frank for money. Once he wanted a loan for a new car; then he needed two hundred thousand dollars for a medical procedure. A few days before he died, he left a message on Frank's voice mail that he needed thirty thousand dollars, for what he didn't say. Frank didn't call him back. The next he heard, Trip was dead. The police didn't find Trip in a ditch, as I had been told; they discovered his body on the floor of his apartment. Nor was he buried in a pauper's field. More than four hundred people, including several of our classmates, attended his funeral.

His obituary mentioned how he had competed in the Boston, New York, and Cleveland marathons. The reporter depicted him as being a tenacious, competitive go-getter. But the paragraph that struck me most was the one that described him as being "a purveyor of practical jokes, one-liners and funny stories. As his sister said: 'Trip never forgot a punch line to a joke. He would drop by a friend's office and tell the receptionist he was from the IRS.'"

Trip could be a charmer but he had demons too; otherwise he wouldn't have made such a mess of his life. Trip became a bully because that's what miserable people do to feel less miserable about themselves: They make other people miserable.

When Frank said he couldn't understand why I was so obsessed with his friend, he had a good point. Before I could get on with my life, I needed to understand why I had reacted so strongly to Trip and why I had allowed him to occupy such a prominent place in my psyche.

IT WASN'T EASY for me to look back. I felt like an emotional wreck in high school, and an outsider too. My father had lost his job and I was one of three scholarship students in my class. I was also one of the few Jews. I had won the middle school's scholar/athlete award, so my teachers, parents, and coaches had high expectations for me. But I let them down. I started both ways on the varsity football team, but I made a lot more fumbles than touchdowns my sophomore year and got badly hurt. I was the starting pitcher on the varsity baseball team and had a 1.20 earned run average, but that summer I threw out my arm on the GO team, ending my dreams of getting a college scholarship. It seemed that I spent more time in emergency rooms than on the ball field.

Because I was so insecure and primed for other catastrophes to occur, I saw anti-Semitism where it wasn't and turned Trip into my Idi Amin. I fantasized about getting my revenge, including the sweetest type of all: to become so successful that he'd never be able to hurt me again or expose me for being a failure, fraud, and has-been.

I imagine now that Trip must have been plagued by similar fears. If I had understood this at the time, I might have responded differently to him. Perhaps I would have simply taken my hit on the football field and walked away, without any paranoid thoughts. That would have been quite a feat for a fifteen-year-old kid—for someone at any age.

IT'S FUNNY, OR maybe it's understandable, that so many of the feelings I experienced after losing my job mirrored the ones I had in reaction to Trip and his co-conspirator, Dave, after they bloodied me during the scrimmage. I felt manipulated and excluded by the people who had cut me off at the legs without warning or explanation. I had trusted them and given them my best efforts. I had looked to them to protect me. Why had they been so calculating and cruel?

I could picture my former colleagues huddled around the chairman's desk congratulating themselves on having made such a tough decision.

Forty years earlier, I had pictured Trip and Dave congratulating themselves on a job well done after I walked dazed and bloodied off the football field.

For weeks after I lost my job, I kept reliving the moment I was fired. The conversation that occurred between me and my managers had been one-sided. The only words I contributed were "What?

You must be kidding." But now, with the luxury of hindsight, I could hold my own with wit and speak truth to power. And just as I had with Trip, I craved revenge. I fantasized about my former bosses walking into their offices one morning and getting *their* comeuppance, as swiftly and coldly as I had gotten mine.

But instead of getting my antagonists out of my mind, my vengefulness only served to strengthen their hold on me. I'd wake up in the middle of the night preoccupied with the people who played a part in my firing. Night and day, I spent far too much time listening to their voices in my head.

THEN ONE MORNING I got a phone call that put the voices I was hearing into perspective. It was from an old girlfriend named Melody whom I hadn't talked with in more than twenty years. Melody had been one of the major loves of my life. She was five years older than I was and she'd always reminded me of Annie Hall, the character Diane Keaton played in the Woody Allen movie. Melody looked like Annie, dressed like Annie, and had Annie's quirky, self-deprecating humor. And like Annie, she was a woman of the 1970s: She believed that she deserved to "have it all," including a partner attuned to everything she needed. I didn't disagree. But it took four painful years for me to understand that I would never become the partner she wanted me to be without becoming somebody I absolutely wasn't.

It was good hearing from Melody again, and kismet catching up. Since our last encounter, she had moved from Cleveland to Germany, studied at the Jung Institute in Zurich, earned her Ph.D. in clinical psychology, and become a psychoanalyst. She would turn sixty in a year, and she was thinking of moving back to Cleveland so that she could become more involved in the lives of her nieces, her nephews, and her own son. She told me she intended to take care of some of her own unfinished business.

I was particularly intrigued to hear that Melody's Ph.D. thesis had been on the topic of forgiveness, which was so central to the process of making amends. When I asked her why she had chosen this topic, she told me that she had been struggling at the time to forgive her mother, who was dying, and also her boyfriend, whom she characterized as being "insufficiently attentive."

She said her breakthrough came when she realized that the two struggles were related. "When my boyfriend didn't listen to me, when he kept turning away, he ripped open my oldest and deepest wound, the one that my mother had inflicted on me when I was a child by being so distant and cold. It enraged me."

I remembered being the target of Melody's rage when we were dating: She would sit up in bed or leave a party, accusing me, too, of not being attentive to her needs. I would react badly. I would sulk, get drunk, or blame her for being self-important and impossible to please.

I was anxious to hear more about Melody's breakthrough.

"Once, as we were sitting across from each other, my boyfriend said something really insensitive and I just froze up and drifted away," she said. "Suddenly, I had this image of a tiny frozen baby who had been thrown from its crib. The baby was lying on the floor, abandoned and alone. The image haunted me. And then I realized, 'That frozen baby is in me. It's an essential part of myself that I have been ignoring. I need to listen to it and take care of it.' Once I understood that, I was able to forgive my boyfriend and turn my attention to the part of me that I had neglected."

Melody spoke so gently and with such compassion that I sensed she had forgiven not only her boyfriend and her mother but also herself and everyone else who had been "insufficiently attentive" to her needs, including me. And there were other qualities I noticed in her that had not been apparent when we dated: She was both humble and generous in sharing what she had learned. Half a lifetime ago, when she was my girlfriend, she would jump from one new age fad to another, touting each new discovery as "the One

True Way." But it was clear that the self-knowledge she had gained had both deepened and mellowed her.

Melody had committed herself to the arduous process of being a more self-aware person and her hard work had paid off. She had discovered what she called "the neglected, shamed shadow part" of herself, and she had begun taking care of it. I sensed that I could trust her in a way that I hadn't before. And so I told her how diminished I still felt from losing my job—and how I couldn't sleep at night, and about my longing for revenge.

"It's as if you're possessed," she said, referring to the way my condition would have been labeled in the Middle Ages. "It's as if your soul has been occupied by the devil, right?"

"Yeah," I said. "It's as if they've taken up residence in my psyche. How do I get them out?"

"Brain surgery," she laughed.

"No, really," I said.

"What you really need to do is walk into the muck and feel all the feelings that are persecuting you, all the fear, confusion, and pain. That's the first step," she said. "The next step is to get curious about those uncomfortable feelings and ask yourself, 'Where are they coming from? Where is all this jealousy and hatred and this sense of being abandoned and misunderstood coming from?' For me, the anger I had toward my boyfriend was a response to an earlier trauma. Once I could recognize that, I was on the path to forgiveness. It's tricky stuff. That's why I advise people to go to people like me for guidance."

"So getting fired reminded me of an earlier trauma in my life, which brought out some of my same fears and insecurities and similar feelings of revenge."

"Right."

"So what comes next?"

"You need to fess up," she said. "Instead of focusing on how your bosses betrayed and victimized you, look at your own behavior.

What role did *you* play in your getting fired? Is there something *you* could have done that would have led to a different outcome?"

"Then what?"

"If you can say to yourself, 'I'm tired of being tortured and I want to stop the pain' and really mean it, then you're ready to forgive both the people who wronged you and yourself."

"But how do you know that you've been successful?" I asked.

"Little by little, you realize that you are feeling neutral instead of inflamed. The malice, the voices, the vengeful fantasies grow less intense. They quiet down; then they're gone."

My hour with Melody was up. Back in Berlin, one of her other patients, a paying one, was waiting to see her.

MELODY GAVE ME another way to think about the voices in my head. It was clear that my anger at my bosses echoed the feelings I had experienced forty years earlier with Trip, and that those feelings might be traced to an even earlier trauma in my life. It was also clear that I deserved at least some of the blame for getting fired. I could have done a better job of communicating to my bosses that their goals were mine. I could have made more compromises. I could have been less stiff-necked and proud.

Melody was right: When you recognize your own role in the crimes against you, you can't be as militant in your call for revenge.

But why had I gotten myself into the bind in the first place? Wasn't that an even bigger and more basic question?

For reasons that were becoming clearer to me, I had put on blinders at work. I didn't want to see or believe the signs that my days there were numbered. If I had been more attuned to the reality of my situation, I would have started to look for another job. I would have gone on interviews and made my availability known to headhunters long before my bosses even had a chance to fire me. Instead, I left my fate in the hands of people who had their reasons for no longer favoring me. Had I not put the blinders on, I would have worked less hard at my job and focused more of my energy on figuring out what came next. Instead, I worked harder and harder until I wore myself down and became even more of a stranger to my children.

Melody's breakthrough came after she discovered a baby who was frozen and abandoned inside of herself. If there was a baby inside of me, he was comically sad, like the assembly-line worker Charlie Chaplin played in *Modern Times*. I imagined my inner baby walking on a treadmill at the same time he is lifting weights and trying to read a newspaper. The treadmill starts going faster and faster, but because he doesn't have any hands free, he's unable to adjust the dial to a lower setting.

I had allowed my fears of change and failure to get in the way of figuring out what I wanted to do in my life. Those same fears had led me to work so hard and zealously that I lost sight of what mattered most, resulting in a huge pile of emotional loose ends. I was making progress, though. My unfinished business with Trip had led me closer to a place where I could forgive my bosses and myself. The voices weren't gone yet, but they were quieting down.

In my favorite scene in *Annie Hall*, Alvy Singer runs into Annie on a Manhattan street corner a few months after they have broken up for good. The tension that pushed them apart is surprisingly gone. The two ex-lovers have a wonderful conversation and think warm thoughts about each other. Then they go their separate ways.

That's how I felt talking to Melody after all these years. She was as charming, funny, and brilliant as I remembered her being when we dated each other. I was happy to hear that she had achieved professional success, and even happier that she had found and begun nurturing her abandoned inner baby. She was humble and generous and she gave me a gift for which I'll always be grateful: the image of my own inner vulnerability. Going forward, I would need to protect myself from becoming overwhelmed and losing perspective on my life.

CHAPTER SIX

Thank You, Mr. Jarvis

Seeking Spiritual Guidance from a Mentor

HIS NAME WAS Rev. F. Washington Jarvis III, Tony for short, and he couldn't have come into my life at a more critical time. The once-successful company my grandfather founded had been sold for a pittance. My father, who had been its president, was unemployed. My parents could no longer pay for tuition, and so I became one of the few scholarship students at the boys' school I attended.

My mother had married into a well-off family but now she was working as a telemarketer, interviewing people who were wealthier than she was about products she could no longer afford. She was mortified by her change in financial status, and afraid. And then her father, my grandpa Bert, died way too young, depriving us of yet another source of comfort and security in what had suddenly become a harsh world.

My father, the optimist, pretended that everything was fine; my mother was convinced that we were about to be homeless; and we, their children, were caught in the middle, not knowing which of our parents to believe.

When the mailman would arrive each day, my father was always there to greet him; that way, he could get to the bills first and hide them from my mother. At night, while my father slept, my mother would come downstairs and suggest that she regretted ever marrying him—a confession I both resented and feared. That was my life at home. At school, my confidence had been eroded by a series of setbacks and injuries and by my ego-deflating bully, Trip.

Enter Father Jarvis, a twenty-nine-year-old Episcopal minister who had gone to Harvard College, Cambridge University, and the Episcopal Theological School at Harvard. Not only was he the best-educated person I had ever met, he was handsome and self-confident, and when he walked into the classroom in his preacher's collar, with his sleeves rolled up, we used to joke that God was in the room, which he didn't dispute.

Father Jarvis made the courses he taught seem not only essential and profound but cool. We studied Aristotle, Socrates, Buber, and Freud. We read all four Gospels of the New Testament and also Sartre and Camus. We wrote papers on the psychology of the Nazis and on the meaning of love. We debated Ayn Rand's critique of altruism and the existence and nature of God.

Those heady discussions provided a respite from the pain and heartbreak I confronted each night at home. They also inspired me to study history, write fiction, tutor inner-city kids, and set my sights on attending an Ivy League college.

Father Jarvis exposed me to great writers and big ideas, but he also inspired me by seeing talents and qualities in me that I didn't see in myself. During my senior year, he asked me to edit and proofread the manuscript of a book he was writing on Christianity. I will always cherish what he wrote in the acknowledgments section of his book: "Lee Richard Kravitz read the entire final manuscript with extreme care and suggested many improvements." The fact that a teacher I respected took me and my comments seriously helped me become more serious about myself.

So why, when I left for college, did I neglect to thank Mr. Jarvis for transforming my sense of myself? Was it because I knew that other students would soon replace me as his favorite? And why didn't I stay in touch with him once I had achieved a modicum of success? Was it because I felt that, whatever I accomplished, I could never live up to the promise he had seen in me?

I wanted to see Father Jarvis again so I could make amends for not thanking him. And, after losing my job, it would be nice to reconnect with someone who had bolstered my confidence at an earlier stage in my life.

I got his address and wrote to him. He wrote back that he was delighted to hear from me. He had just started a new job at Yale's Berkeley Divinity School in New Haven. But he would be back in Boston in early December to give a series of lectures on medieval architecture, and he invited me to stay at his flat while we caught up and talked about what he referred to as "our" unfinished business.

THE HIGH-SPEED ACELA train from Penn Station, New York, to South Station, Boston, takes three hours and fifty-five minutes. I spent that time reading two essays I had written in high school and a book of sermons that Father Jarvis had given in the 1980s and 1990s while he was headmaster of a private boys' school in Boston.

My first essay, "Is Love Practical in Real Life?", was bloodied by Tony's red markings. He found sections of my essay "clumsy, pretentious, extraneous." My generalizations were "doubtful, irrelevant, and wide-eyed." In eighteen pages there were only three "goods" and one "Yes!" Father Jarvis had *hated* my essay on love.

"That Which Frustration Breeds: Comparisons in the Psychological Development of the Racial Doctrines in Nazism and Black Muslim-ism" fared better. The responses "awkward," "non sequitur," and "unclear" appeared in the margins a number of times. Father Jarvis called one statement "a great oversimplification" and another "too sweeping." But in the end he wrote, "A superb job and triumphant end to a great year for you, Lee." And he gave me an A.

I can only imagine how shocked I must have felt when I saw that grade. Why? Because, of all my teachers, Mr. Jarvis demanded the most of his students. How many teachers take the time to rip apart and challenge their students' thinking in this era of crowded classrooms, inflated grades, and teaching to the test?

WE ALSO LIVE in a secular era, which is why the title of Tony's book, *With Love and Prayers: A Headmaster Speaks to the Next Generation*, struck me as quaint. Roxbury Latin, the school he had headed for thirty years, was founded in 1649. This made it the oldest school in continuous existence in the United States. Roxbury's average SAT scores were the highest in the nation; no high school had a higher percentage of its students matriculating at Harvard, Stanford, and MIT.

For such a tiny school, less than three hundred students in grades seven through twelve, Roxbury Latin was unusually diverse, the result of its substantial endowment, which allowed a needs-blind acceptance policy. But, according to the Reverend Peter J. Gomes, in the introduction to Tony's book, the real key to Roxbury Latin's success was its anachronistic headmaster—"an unrepentant Episcopal clergyman" who was more concerned with building character and leaders than with grades, and "who prays for his boys and tells them that he loves them, and in public, regularly."

Tony Jarvis's sermons were full of tough-love homilies, such as "The only life worth living is the hard life" and "Happiness comes from caring more about others than you care about yourself." There was nothing meek or mild about Tony's approach. In another sermon he told his boys, "If your generation is like those that have gone before it—and it is the majority of your contemporaries will choose unreflective, shallow, comfortable, self-indulgent existences. They will be copies." Instead, he urged, "Don't be a copy. Be a captain of your own destiny."

And he ended his book with the following prayer:

My dear children, now and in the years ahead you will suffer
and fail and know despair. My prayer for you is that when you
experience such suffering you will dig deep and from your suffering build the spiritual muscle you will need to cope with
life's many difficulties, and that in your own suffering you will
grow to understand with compassion the suffering of others.

Strangely, as I read those words on the train, I felt that they were
directed to me. In the forty years since I'd seen my mentor, had
I dug deep enough, in *my* times of trouble, to build the spiritual
muscle I needed to lead a life of courage and compassion?

THE ACELA LEFT me at South Station and from there I took the
Red Line to Ashmont. Then I boarded the Mattapan High Speed
Trolley and took it three stops to Milton. Following Tony's instructions, I exited the trolley, crossed a pair of railway tracks, and climbed
a tall stairway into the snow.

I paused to get my bearings. The part of Dorchester where I was
standing was called Lower Mills, and Tony lived across the street
and two blocks away in a condominium complex that had once been
the headquarters of Baker's Chocolate, the country's first chocolate
manufacturer. As I walked in the snow toward the redbrick building, I could imagine the delight that Tony must have taken in the
Neponset River, only a dozen yards away, gleaming in the moonlight.

I pressed the buzzer, got let in, and then took the "lift," as Tony
called it, up to his floor.

He poked his head out the door: "Welcome, welcome. I thought
you'd never make it." He grabbed my arm and ushered me through
the door. "What would you like to drink—beer, wine, or scotch?"

"What are you having?" I asked.

"Scotch on the rocks, splash of water."

"Me too," I said, wondering, like a kid again, whether it would have been more grammatical for me to have said, "Pour two."

In the dim light of the dining room Tony looked much the same as I had remembered him but older: trim and fit, with the thin, sharp features of a British aristocrat. I had expected him to greet me in a stiff clerical collar, but instead he wore an open-necked blue shirt under a beige cotton sweater. Most of Tony's remaining hair was still blond, and he kept combing it off his forehead with his fingertips, just as he used to. I had last seen him when he was thirty; he was nearly seventy years old.

"I told myself that I'd just relax, travel, and write after I retired," he said. "But I can't stop working."

Since leaving Roxbury in 2004, Tony had taught and lectured in Australia, New Zealand, and South Africa. He had also served two terms as a chaplain and master at Eton College, the famous boys' school in England. "Between the teaching, advising, and pastoral duties," he said, "I got so tired I scared myself."

In the spring of 2008, Tony returned to Dorchester to begin his retirement. But before he could unpack his suitcases, the head of Yale's Berkeley Divinity School called, asking if he would be interested in starting a new program for chaplains and religion teachers who wanted to work in schools. It was a job he couldn't turn down. So now, on the cusp of his seventieth birthday, he was sleeping four nights a week in a college dorm room in New Haven and the other three nights in Dorchester, where he still served as an associate priest at All Saints Church. "I live like a vagabond," he said, as he started toward the kitchen to fix our drinks. "But really, I love what I'm doing and it's wonderful to see you again. Please, make yourself comfortable."

I DID. TONY's living room walls were papered the deepest red and blue I had seen outside of a five-star hotel. There was a couch, two antique chairs, fresh-cut flowers on the tables, and a handsome Persian rug. The furniture was arranged for civilized conversation, not for entertaining or little kids.

On one wall there were eight bookshelves, with about five hundred books per shelf. They were divided by topic into theology, philosophy, psychology, and history. Most of the novelists Tony read were British. There were several hundred biographies of great men and at least two dozen books about private boys' schools, including the two he had written about Roxbury Latin. From the cracks on their covers, it seemed that the majority of the books in Tony's library had been read.

Tony reentered the room with our drinks.

"Before we start catching up, I want to thank you for being such an important figure in my life," I said. Then I raised my glass. "Here's to great teachers. And to you, Tony, for believing in me when I needed you most."

"Cheers," he reciprocated, and we took a sip of scotch.

"You know, Lee, it's nice of you to thank me but it's not something I either need or expect," he said. "I've probably taught fifteen hundred boys over the years, and only a fraction of them have ever thanked me."

"Wasn't 'thank you' one of the 'three phrases to live by' that you prescribed in your book, along with 'I'm wrong' and 'I'm sorry'?"

"Sure," Tony said. "You should always thank people when you feel grateful. Whenever you say 'thank you,' you affirm a person's existence."

"But never expect people to thank *you*," I said.

"Exactly," he said. "Expect gratitude and you start doing things for the wrong reason. Expect gratitude and you'll be disappointed." Then he paused for a second. "I want to get back to something else you said."

"What's that?" I asked.

"The amount of encouragement you thought you needed from me in high school. Was your confidence in yourself so low?"

"Yes," I said. "I was an emotional basket case." I told Tony how my father had lost his job and how my arm and dreams had been shattered. And I confessed how estranged I felt being a Jew and a scholarship kid at such a wealthy, Waspish school.

"I had no idea," he said.

"You didn't?" I said, remembering how certain I had been that everyone at the school knew about my problems. Mr. Jarvis, I'd figured, would have been the teacher most attuned to my angst; he would have recognized my pain and tried to ease it. Wasn't that the main reason he took me under wing?

"No," he said. "I always thought you were smart, mature, and open to new ideas. I thought you were the perfect student."

"*Me?*" I said. Either I had misread the situation back in high school or Tony was kidding me. "*You* were the perfect one. Wasn't it you who was sent to earth to save adolescents like me from killing themselves?"

"Yeah, Superpriest," he laughed. "Born on Krypton, raised in Greenwich, and schooled on the fields of Dover. Is that what you thought?"

"Something like that," I said.

"Well, the truth is, I was born in Pittsburgh and raised in Painesville. I went to public school until I got a scholarship to go to boarding school, which I hated at first but loved when I gained some confidence. You know about Harvard and Cambridge. But when I first met you I was earning thirty-six hundred dollars a year as an associate pastor at a church in suburban Cleveland. I ran an underfunded youth ministry that attracted hundreds of kids. Most of the kids were smoking pot or worse. It was the sixties. The girls were getting pregnant and the boys were doing everything they could to get out of fighting in Vietnam. They were scared and angry and I took them to the poorest section of Cleveland to tutor impoverished black kids.

"I loved all of them, the rich kids and the poor ones, and because I wanted to understand and serve them better, I started to go to a shrink. I went five times a week for five years for classical lie-down-on-the-couch Freudian analysis, and it ate up everything I earned. That's when the headmaster of University School offered me a thousand dollars per month to teach a course in philosophy. Because I had to eat and pay my rent, I said yes."

"I had no idea," I said.

"So neither of us had any idea what was going on in the other person's life. Well, now we do," he laughed. "Tomorrow we can pick up where we left off in eleventh grade." He handed me a twelve-page double-spaced manuscript. "Here's your homework assignment," he said. It was titled "On Death's Row," and I read it in the quiet of my bedroom before falling asleep.

TONY HAD GIVEN the sermon the previous week, on the first Sunday of Advent. His inspiration had come from Mark 13:33: "Take heed, watch, for you know not when the time will come."

I could picture Tony standing on the pulpit in his priestly attire, looking down at this text, then up at his parishioners.

"I have been thinking about what we Christians call The Four Last Things—death, judgment, heaven and hell—a lot recently. And I have decided to speak about death this morning."

Why death? On Monday a friend had called to tell him that her husband had just died of a massive heart attack while playing squash. On Tuesday he had dinner with a colleague whose mother-in-law was about to die. On Wednesday he drove to New Hampshire to see his beloved former assistant, who had just been diagnosed with Alzheimer's.

"When I was a boy in Ohio, many a family had an old grandmother or grandfather living in the same house," he told his parishioners. "My friends and I, as children, saw people grow old and infirm and sometimes senile, and we saw them die. Death was part of our lives.

"It is not usually so today," he said. "We live in a society—in a time—that is terrified of death, that denies death. Many of our contemporaries cannot even say the word 'death.' People routinely say 'she passed away,' or, more often now, 'she passed.'"

The Reverend F. Washington Jarvis then told the story of a man who had spent fifteen years on death row for a crime he didn't commit. Was the man angry? No. "We are all on death row," the man had told interviewer Studs Terkel. "The only difference is that when you're in prison, it's the state that decides when you die."

"Delbert Tibbs, the wrongly accused prisoner, was right," Tony said. "We are all on death row. And if you seek to discover the meaning of your life, you have to begin with the one and only thing you can say for certain about your life: You will die. We are all on death row and we are all dying. And that reality should awaken in each of us a sense of urgency."

I could see Tony pausing for effect, then directing his next comments to the younger people in the pews. He told them that the next two weeks would bring the anniversaries of the murders of two boys from the parish. One of the boys had been killed by a mentally disturbed man as he waited to board a plane in Rome. The other had been stabbed to death when he came to the defense of a girl he did not know. "We are warned, in this Gospel season, that death comes like a thief in the night," Tony said. Then he repeated Mark 13:33: "Take heed, watch, for you know not when the time will come."

Tony addressed his closing remarks to all of us, to the 250 or so individuals who had come to his church that morning and to the millions of people, including you and me, who had not. "We live under the illusion that we are here on earth forever," he said. "But

Advent warns us that our time on earth is short, that our time is running out. So while we have time," he said slowly, "let us consider what we want to make of it."

I PUT THE sermon down. I had heard a version of it nearly forty years ago, in Father Jarvis's philosophy class. At the time we were reading the essays and novels of Albert Camus, the French existentialist. My favorite, *The Myth of Sisyphus*, featured a Greek mythological figure who was condemned to roll a boulder up a steep hill, only to have it roll back down, again and again, forever. To Camus, Sisyphus signified the absurdity of human existence.

Which raised a pretty basic question: If life is pointless, how (or even why) should we live? Camus weighed three options in *The Myth of Sisyphus*: commit suicide, take a leap of faith toward God, or accept life's absurdity and create your own meaning. I couldn't remember the arguments pro and con for each option, but I did recall Camus' own conclusion: Accept life's absurdity and create your own meaning.

"The struggle itself . . . is enough to fill a man's heart," he wrote. "One must imagine Sisyphus happy."

Or as Tony had sermonized: "We are on Death's Row. Our time is running out. Let us consider what we want to make of it."

WHAT HAD I made of my own brief time on earth? Had I imbued my life with meaning?

It certainly looked that way on paper. I had traveled to more than forty countries and experienced a good sampling of the world's cultures. I had decided to become a journalist so I could use my reporting to educate and inspire people. I had become a magazine editor so I could help other journalists tell stories that made a difference in people's lives. I had led projects and campaigns and served on the boards of organizations that moved millions of Americans to volunteer and take action for the betterment of their communities and the world.

On paper, I had constructed a meaning-filled life for myself. So why didn't it feel that way? Perhaps I had chosen the wrong way to pursue it. By working so hard, by focusing on every little detail, by letting my perfectionism hold sway, I had given short shrift to what truly mattered: my wife and children and friends. As good as my life looked on paper, it was sorely lacking in the one area that puts flesh on meaning: human connectedness. I had experienced the power of that when I reached out to Fern and Akmal and other important people from my past. But I knew I would struggle to incorporate this into my life on an ongoing basis. What would it take for me to achieve a more connected life? Perhaps my old mentor, Father Jarvis, would have some clues.

BY THE TIME I woke up and made my way into the dining room, Tony had gone out to buy the morning papers and left them on the table for my enjoyment. The big news was that 550,000 Americans had lost their jobs during the previous month, and analysts were predicting the worst holiday retail season in thirty-five years. The Yankees were about to spend $140 million to get a new pitcher. And Detroit's big three automakers were begging Congress to bail them out with $35 billion in loans. The news from abroad was equally disturbing: terrorist attacks in Mumbai and more chest-pounding and posturing from Putin.

"I'll put on a fresh pot of coffee," Tony said. "How did you sleep?"

"Okay," I said. "But I kept dreaming about a guy named Sisyphus."

"Was he rolling a rock?" Tony asked.

"He was," I said. "Do you know him?"

"Not personally," Tony laughed. "But he's shown up at a couple of my lectures over the years."

"I read your 'On Death's Row' sermon last night," I said.

"And?"

"It led me back to eleventh-grade philosophy class. To the idea that death is the starting point for any discussion about the meaning of life."

"Very good," he smiled. "You get an A, Lee. You also get one of your teacher's perfectly toasted English muffins," he said, handing me a muffin, the butter, and a dish of strawberry jam.

"Thank you," I said.

I buttered the muffin. Then I got back to my dream. "I was playing halfback in a big game against Gilmour. The quarterback kept handing me the ball on Gilmour's ten-yard line; I kept fumbling it on the two. I felt like Sisyphus, running as hard as I could, over and over again, only I kept fumbling, for eternity."

"Did that ever happen to you in a game?" he asked. "Did you ever blow your chance to be a hero?"

"All the time," I said. "And, in part, I blame you. After reading Camus in your philosophy class, I couldn't stay focused on anything I was supposed to do. I questioned everything: 'Why am I hurling my body into this sea of bullies? Why am I submitting myself to so much pain? Why, in the locker room before a game, am I saying the Lord's Prayer?' You have to admit that high school football looks pretty absurd through the prism of *The Stranger*. Why did you do that to us?"

"Do what?"

"Why did you get us questioning everything, including the meaning of life itself, at such an impressionable age?"

"Because you were doing it anyway," Tony said. He put down his coffee and looked straight at me. "In every generation adolescents are thirsting—whether they know it or admit it—for answers to the question of who they are, where they fit in, whether their lives have any meaning or purpose. I taught Camus because I believed in his view of the universe and wanted to clear out all that juvenile claptrap in your head."

"What claptrap do you mean?"

"For example, the idea that there's a big daddy in the sky who rewards you when you're good and punishes you when you're bad. Guess what, kiddies? Life isn't fair."

That line bugged me in high school and it annoyed me now. I also hated it when Tony narrowed his eyes and said that humankind was born "mean, nasty, and brutish"—a phrase he lifted, in part, from the English philosopher Thomas Hobbes.

"Do you still think so little of human nature?" I asked. "Do you still think we are 'mean, nasty, and brutish,' or whatever your buddy Hobbes said?"

"What do you think?" he asked as he handed me the front page of that day's *New York Times*. "Scratch any of us and beneath the surface is a murderer or destroyer. I think Rousseau's idea that man is good in the state of nature, that it's society that makes us bad, is ridiculous," he said dismissively. "We're mean and we're thuggish. That's why education exists—to take us out of our selfish little selves and civilize us."

In philosophy class that year, we spent a great deal of time talking about the Holocaust. Tony had been a child of World War II, and I was a member of the generation of American Jews that had been born in the decade after six million Jews had been exterminated in Nazi death camps. Tony saw the Holocaust as Hobbes run wild. My grandparents saw it as evidence that the world hated Jews and would kill us again unless we had our own state in Israel.

I had been confused. After I saw my first film about the death camps when I was thirteen, I put a pillow over my face until I could barely breathe. I wanted to experience the horror to which the Nazis had subjected their victims. In my heart, though, I wanted to believe that the Nazis were an aberration, that human beings were essentially good.

We read William Shirer's *The Rise and Fall of the Third Reich*, Hitler's *Mein Kampf*, and Eric Hoffer's *The True Believer* in that class. But the book that had the biggest impact on me was *Man's Search for Meaning* by the Austrian-born psychiatrist Viktor Frankl.

Frankl's wife had been murdered at Auschwitz, and so had his parents, but Frankl survived and he devoted his life to studying the effects of brutality and extreme suffering on the human mind. Frankl concluded that human beings seek meaning even in the worst of circumstances. He was particularly heartened by those prisoners "who walked through the huts comforting others, giving away their last piece of bread. They may have been few in number," he wrote, "but they offer sufficient proof that everything can be taken from a man but one thing: the last of the human freedoms—to choose one's attitude in any given set of circumstances, to choose one's own way."

I thought about the 550,000 Americans who had just lost their jobs, the families mourning the victims of the terrorist bombs in Mumbai, the refugees left homeless from the fighting in Gaza, the Sudan, and Iraq, the heartaches and tragedies afflicting most of the human race each and every day, and the one that afflicts all of us—the fact that we will die. How should we respond?

In the face of what he called the "benign indifference of the universe," Camus said, Create your own meaning.

Frankl said, Choose your own way.

And Jarvis quoted Jesus, who said, "Ye shall have tribulation."

"It would be wrong to give young people the impression that there is no pain in life," Tony said as he drove me from his flat in Dorchester to the idyllic, 120-acre campus of the school he had headed in West Roxbury. Then he added, with stoic certainty, "It is through our trials and tribulation that we discover our inner strength and what will give our life its meaning."

TONY PARKED THE car and hurried me into a side entrance. He was anxious to test the projector and go through his slides before his lecture began, and when the projector didn't work (does it ever at first?), he confronted the first major test that day of his inner strength. "Who can help me here?" he said in an imperious, somebody-better-get-this-right-and-I-mean-now voice. A teacher ran for the school's tech guy, who rushed back and flicked a switch that Tony had over-looked. Tony loosened his clerical collar, and both the teacher and tech guy suppressed their chuckles.

The boys had started to file through the door to take their seats. There was no school uniform, but most of the boys were wearing long-sleeved polo shirts with horizontal stripes, and either khaki pants or jeans with tennis shoes.

Tony peered down at his notes, then up at his audience of fifteen-year-old boys.

"From our previous lectures," he said, "let us remember that Europe's great Gothic cathedrals were built as offerings to God."

He showed a slide of Notre Dame in Paris.

"This great and towering example of Gothic architecture was built more than seven hundred years ago to honor an inconsequen-tial Jewish girl who bore her child in a stable. These flying buttresses were erected to keep the cathedral's walls from cracking under the weight of its stained-glass windows. But notice how they have the effect of lifting the cathedral and our spirit toward heaven.

"Mystical on the inside, rational on the outside, this great cathe-dral is a place of historical and religious importance." he continued. "On state occasions, it displays the 'Crown of Thorns' that Jesus wore on Calvary. It was here that Henry VI of England was crowned king of France and Mary, Queen of Scots, got married to Henry II's son. Napoleon crowned himself emperor here. And who can tell me the name of the modern French leader whose final requiem was held at Notre Dame?"

"Was it de Gaulle?" one boy asked.

"Yes, very good," Tony said. "It was General Charles de Gaulle, the father of modern France."

Tony's next slide showed Notre Dame's west facade, with its three large portals. "Can anyone tell me what's odd about these doors?" he asked.

"It's like they're . . ." one boy began.

"Like?" Father Jarvis said. "They're not 'like' anything."

Everyone but the offending boy laughed.

"The door on the right is open," another boy said. "The doors to the other two are closed."

"Doors tend to do that. They open and close," Tony said. "Anyone else?"

"They aren't the same size," a boy offered timidly.

"Right," Father Jarvis exulted. "They're not symmetrical. The Greeks loved symmetry, but the French thought symmetry was boring."

Tony started to pick up steam.

Of the central portal's depiction of the Last Judgment, he said, "Look at the holes in Christ's hands. There is a great longing in us for justice to be done, and here is a judge who has experienced the worst possible pain and torture we humans can bear. He is a judge who understands us."

Of a frieze depicting Mary's death and ascension to heaven, he asked, "Why is Mary called the ark?" He tried another tact. "Remember the Old Testament. What purpose did the ark serve in the First and Second Temples?"

"It carried the word of God," said a boy.

"So I ask you again: Why is Mary called the ark?"

"Because, as the mother of Jesus, Mary bore God into the world," the boy said.

"Yes," Tony said. He looked at his watch and saw that he had time for one last slide. He skipped through several to get to an image of Notre Dame's famous rose window. On the balustrade below the window, there was an engraving of the Virgin and Child, flanked by two angels.

"From street level, what does the window look like?" he asked.

"A halo," said a boy who himself looked like an angel.

"And what does the halo in its circularity convey?"

"The eternal," said the boy.

"That's right," said Tony. "Thus, in this image of the Virgin and Child enshrined in the halo, we see the eternal in the midst of the worldly. And in this great cathedral, we see heaven brought to earth and earth to heaven." He placed both hands on the lectern. "Tomorrow, we will visit another great cathedral—Chartres." The bell rang. "Class dismissed."

As the boys filed out of the classroom, Tony took his glasses off and rubbed the bridge of his nose. He didn't need to give these lectures, but he did it anyway and partly because he thought no one could give them better. But I could also see that this annual lecture series was one of the many Sisyphean boulders that Tony would roll up hills for the rest of his life. Most of these boys wouldn't visit the cathedrals of Notre Dame, Chartres, or Salisbury for years, if ever. And when they did, their own teenage kids would be bugging them to leave. But Tony would keep pushing this boulder forever, in a one-man effort to keep at least the possibility of Western civilization alive. As it was for Sisyphus, the struggle itself was enough to fill Tony's heart. One must imagine Mr. Jarvis happy.

ACTUALLY, DURING MY three days at his side, Tony seemed happiest by far when he was sauntering through his old school's halls. Whenever he encountered a boy, he would grab the boy's arm and give him a shoulder butt. Walking through Roxbury Latin with Tony was like being in a bumper car at an amusement park.

"Hi, John," he would say. Bump. "Heard from Middlebury yet?"

"No, Mr. Jarvis."

"Call me when you do."

"How's it going, Bill?" Bump.

"All right," Bill says. Tony frowns.

Bill corrects himself: "All right, Mr. Jarvis."

"I have a name," Tony says. He looks upward toward the heavens. "I live." He grabs Bill's arm. An extra bump for Bill.

As we turn a corner, Tony stops and shoulder-bumps a boy who is at least 220 pounds of pure muscle.

"Whoa," he says. "You've been lifting, Patrick, haven't you? Are you playing hockey this term?"

"Yes, Mr. Jarvis."

"Will you be a star?"

"I hope so," Patrick says.

"*Be* a star," Tony commands.

"Who loves you the most?" he says to Patrick, as he does to boy after boy.

"You do, Mr. Jarvis," they all say.

Later, I asked Tony about all that shoulder bumping. "Adolescent boys need physical contact," he explained. "You see it when they're walking down the street together, or on the playing field. Physical contact acknowledges their existence. It wakes them up and keeps them in the game."

And how about all those professions of love?

"I've tried to love every boy I've taught as if they're my own child, including you, Lee." He mentioned a boy I'd known in high school. "Remember Charlie?"

"Sure," I said. "He was kind of a goof-off."

"That's right. He wasn't performing anywhere near his potential and I kept pushing and pushing him and he kept resisting my efforts. So I asked him, 'Why do you think I'm doing this?' And he

said, 'Because you love me.' And he was right. I pushed him because I loved him. And he said, 'I wish you didn't,' because he realized how hard it is to live up to another person's love.

"When your love is so deep and selfless that it demands to be
reciprocated, the people you love are forced—for your sake, not
theirs—into becoming better human beings," Tony said.

He was not referring to romantic or filial love, of course. He was
talking about agape, a willed concern for others. Virtually every
holy man in history has considered agape the highest form of love.

"Love takes work," he continued in a soft yet insistent voice. "It
demands that you put yourself in the shoes of another person—and
understand where that person is coming from—before you speak
or act. It requires . . ." He paused for a second and took a deep
breath, as if he were measuring my shoes, to see where I might be
coming from. "It requires that you say, 'I cannot allow you to continue with this behavior,' when a person is acting badly. It means
loving someone selflessly, with no hope or expectation of getting
something in return." He paused again. "Love of this sort can be
inconvenient, unpleasant, costly."

This talk of agape reminded me of another book we read in
Tony's class—*I and Thou*, by the Jewish philosopher Martin Buber.
According to Buber, individuals can experience each other in one of
two ways. In I-It relationships, you encounter people in terms of their
function or category. At work, for example, a person is your boss,
secretary, or coworker. At a doctor's office, you relate to a person as
your internist, nurse, or the receptionist. In an I-Thou relationship,
on the other hand, we experience each other beyond function or category and in our fullness as unique individuals. Take the I-Thou
relationship one step further and you get what the great Christian
philosopher Dietrich Bonhoeffer called "the Beyond-in-the-midst."
It's the idea that we experience God through our relationships with
other human beings.

"Are you still a fan of Buber?" I asked Tony.

"Very much so," Tony said. "Buber understood that nothing of great importance will ever happen between you and me if we view each other as an It. There's a real you that can share yourself with the real me, and we should aspire to that same level of intimacy with God. I think of God all the time. I try to serve God all the time. I ask God's help all the time. I have what I call a 'radical dependency' on God. And that comes from Buber."

BACK IN TONY'S apartment, I asked him, "Why do you need God so much?"

"Everyone dies and nothing lasts." he said. "Yet we long for more, which is why we look to God. The problem is, we are limited as humans and can only experience the transcendent in moments." He quoted from Isaiah: "'"For my thoughts are not your thoughts. Neither are your ways my ways," saith the Lord.'"

I pressed Tony further. "So, even though you can experience only hints of the divine presence, you believe without question in God and would say you have an I-Thou relationship with God?"

"'Believe' is a very bad translation of the Greek," he said. "It should be 'I trust,' as in the phrase 'In God We Trust.' I trust in God. I put all of my money down on God. I also put my hope in God, because our only hope is that God loves us and that his love prevails."

As Tony asserted his belief—or rather, his trust—in God, I found myself envying him. With God in front of him and behind him and protecting his flank, with God as his sword and shield, Tony could face his trials with a lot more confidence than I could. Tony was armed with absolute conviction, while I stood alone and relatively defenseless on the battlefield.

"But how about people like my wife and so many of our friends who don't believe in God at all?" I asked Tony.

"Actually, I think it's better to be a *good* atheist than a *bad* Christian," he said. "If you read the Old Testament and the Hebrew Psalms, the Jewish people struggled time and again with the idea of God, particularly in their times of adversity. The good atheist comes to his atheism after serious consideration. What bothers me are the wishy-washy agnostics who say, 'I don't know and I don't care.'"

I wasn't an atheist or agnostic. But I wasn't a believer yet either. Like the Jews of old, I was struggling with the very idea of God. Those Jews—and Christ himself—felt abandoned by God. "Does God ever forsake you?" I asked Tony.

"I used to think that, but not anymore. I feel empty sometimes—and sapped of energy—but I never feel alone. Praying as I do, I feel that I live each moment in the presence of the saints. And on Sunday, after a hard week, I go to my parish and dump my cares at the foot of Our Lady Mary's shrine."

And then, in a soft but determined voice that filled the room, he quoted another passage from Isaiah: "'They that wait upon the Lord shall renew their strength: They shall mount up with wings as eagles; they shall run and not be weary and they shall walk and not faint.'

"Because I like it so much," he said. "I had a version of that passage inscribed over the entrance to the Jarvis Refectory at the school. It says, 'They that serve the Lord shall renew their strength.'"

In his darkest and most desperate hours, Tony could look to his relationship with God as a source of strength and renewal. Where did I go to dump my cares? More often than not, I ignored them or ran away from them or added them to my pile of unfinished business, where one of the most long-forsaken items was my uncertain relationship with God.

Lately, though, I had found myself praying to someone or something that I increasingly called God. I talked to this God in whispers and shouts, out loud and in my head. I asked it for wisdom when I felt sad and guidance when I felt confused. I thanked it for the happiness I felt when I hugged my aunt Fern and I watched my kids playing with each other. In those moments, I felt myself reaching out to a someone or something far more important and enduring than myself or anything I could imagine. I wanted this something I called God to be more present in my life, particularly as I made amends and reconnected with the people who had mattered most to me. If I really wanted to continue doing the right things in my life, I would need help.

I shared my thoughts with Tony. "I can't say that I trust or even believe in God," I said. "And I don't even call what I'm doing prayer. But whatever I'm doing, these moments comfort me and lift my spirits. Tell me what's going on and how I can do whatever I'm doing better."

Tony paused for a minute before speaking.

"The first thing," he said, "is to stop denying your impulse to pray. Prayer is our deepest human instinct. It begins with the recognition that we are weak and need help. There is so much in life that is beyond our control. So we have to offer up. That's what prayer is: the crying out, the offering up of the mess we're in.

"As to how you can do it better, I have no idea," he said. "I pray all the time, but I'm intuitive and not disciplined at it. The only advice I can give is: Stay open to wherever prayer takes you and it will give you what you need."

BEFORE LEAVING FOR the train station, I wanted to return to the starting place for our discussion—the fact that we all die. How would Tony feel if he discovered that he was going to die, say, tomorrow?

"I'd be okay with it," he said. "In fact I'd welcome it. I'd say, Okay, God, there are some things I've done and there are some things I haven't done, but now it's your turn. I don't believe in heaven and hell; Jesus never said a word about it. But if there's an afterlife—and

I'm not sure there is, Jesus himself tells us not to speculate—I would think it's some sort of place where we can continue to grow spiritually."

From reading his book, I knew that Tony liked to challenge his students at the start of each year by saying, "All of us are going to die—some sooner, some later. After you die, what would you like people to say about you? Your answer to that question," he'd tell them, "should guide the way you live."

So I asked, "After you die, Tony, what would you like people to say about you? And what would you like written on your grave?"

"I really haven't thought about it," he said, with the look of a man who was far from ready to be buried. "But I can tell you what I'd like on the plaque beneath my portrait at Roxbury Latin."

"What's that?" I asked.

"The first line should be 'The Reverend F. Washington Jarvis III.' The second should be '1974–2004,' which are the years I served as headmaster. And then it should say, 'He Loved Us.' That's what I'd like written. 'He loved us.'"

It was time to pack my bags and get going. I stood up to shake Tony's hand and said, "Thank you again for everything."

"Thank you?" he said, faking a furrowed brow. "I thought I told you that I'm not in need of your thanks."

"I wonder if those words don't mean more to you than you let on," I said.

"Maybe they do," he said. "But what I like even more is hearing a teenage boy laugh at one of my jokes, or when I notice an echo of Jarvis in something a boy has said or done."

"Did you notice any of that over the past few days?"

"I did," he said. "And thank you."

THE ACELA FROM South Station, Boston, to Penn Station, New York, took three hours and thirty-five minutes. I spent most of that time recapitulating the highlights of my talks with Tony. I had gone to Boston to thank the savior of my adolescence for lifting my spirits and restoring my confidence during one of the darkest periods of my life. But considerably more had happened over the past three days: The Reverend F. Washington Jarvis III had inspired me again, fortifying my moral framework for whatever lay ahead.

There was nothing soft or sentimental about Tony. In a culture that promised easy paths to wealth, health, and happiness, he was an uncompromising realist: "My dear children, now and in the years ahead you will suffer and fail and know despair." To teenagers who believed they were immortal—and to adults like me, who had lost their way—his message was equally sobering. "If you seek to discover the meaning of your life, you have to begin with the one and only thing you can say for certain about your life: You will die. And that reality should awaken in you a sense of urgency."

That was precisely what I was feeling as I went about taking care of my unfinished business: a sense of urgency. I was fifty-five years old. At any moment I could die, just as quickly and unexpectedly as I had lost my job. My knowledge of that spurred me to make a choice: Instead of rushing to find another job, I had decided to make amends and rekindle my relationships with people I had wronged or neglected. I was pursuing meaning by deepening my connections with other human beings; I was rediscovering my purpose in life and defining work as an activity that enriched me beyond my career.

Love, I was learning, was a big part of it: It was a word that Tony said with astonishing ease. And it was the word that best summarized my trip to Boston. I had gone there to witness and experience one man's agape—his selfless love. It was kind and patient and sought absolutely nothing in return. But it also required an enormous amount of hard work and perseverance. The love that would help me to right my wrongs and be more appreciative of my blessings wasn't the soft-focus, feel-good sort of love: It would take work.

At the beginning of this book, I was a workaholic. I still am. But some things were starting to change.

A year ago, I would have had absolutely no time to consider the question Tony posed to his students at the start of each school year. If you had asked me, "What would you like people to say about you after you die?" I would have said, "I've got no clue."

Now I do. My answer would be something like: "In the end, he worked hardest at love." Those would be excellent words to live by. And if I did let them guide my life, the epitaph on my grave would have a good chance of being: "He completed his unfinished business and lived his life to its fullest."

CHAPTER SEVEN

On the Road to Mount Athos

Taking the Road Not Taken

BY AGE FIFTEEN, my friend Matt was already living in another world. Tall and athletic, with curly blond hair, he had absolutely no interest in cars, dances, or what he considered his parents' soul-numbing lifestyle. What intrigued him most—more even than mathematics and physics, his favorite subjects—were the lives of mystics and holy men.

There was nothing phony about Matt; he was simply more interested than my other friends in all things spiritual. He reminded both me and our classmate Kirk of a character in Hermann Hesse's famous coming-of-age novel, *Demian*, who believed that the world was divided into light and darkness and good and evil and that we should celebrate and find room for both.

Like Demian, Matt urged us to rise above the mentality of the herd and follow the promptings of our own true selves. In the senior yearbook, Kirk described him as being the bird in this passage from Hesse's book:

> *The bird fights its way out of the egg,*
> *The egg is the world.*
> *Who would be born must first destroy a world.*
> *The bird flies to God.*
> *The God's name is Abraxas.*

Abraxas was an ancient god who embodied good and evil. Before Matt could reach Abraxas, he would need to shatter the conventions of the society into which he was born, and Kirk and I intended to be close behind.

FOR OUR SENIOR project in Eastern religions, the three of us took a class in Transcendental Meditation (TM), a technique that was being popularized in the West by followers of the Maharishi Mahesh Yogi.

The class took place at Kent State University in a building adjacent to the green where, twelve months earlier, four students had been shot to death by the Ohio National Guard. Would TM put us on the path to inner and world peace, as the Maharishi had claimed? Would it quiet our minds and expand our worlds? Or would it do absolutely nothing at all?

"We intend to critically evaluate Transcendental Meditation through firsthand experience and by comparing our experiences with at least three other concepts for achieving 'awareness' or 'selflessness.'" That's how the three of us described our project to the faculty committee that okayed it. "We also seek to understand the nature of the 'self,' with the self being equivalent to what Freud calls the 'ego.'"

The Reverend F. Washington Jarvis would have had no stomach for our project, so we took as our adviser an English teacher who had been to India. Looking back, I can't believe that we got away with it. But the three of us were serious. We meditated twice a day and read everything from the Bhagavad Gita to *The Doors of Perception* by Aldous Huxley. When we failed to experience nirvana through TM, we drove to a cabin in Amish country and each took a tab of LSD.

"A lake. A cabin. A meadow. A pretty, rural midwestern sight, but not exactly breathtaking," is how I described the scene in my journal as the acid was beginning to take effect. "But look close. Concentrate on anything. Watch the small patch of rock-covered earth come to life in deep, long breaths. At the core of the world is a giant heart."

The floating green clouds I had seen while meditating with my eyes closed couldn't even remotely compare with the world I was seeing on acid: "Look at a leaf. At any leaf. What you see is a map of the world," I wrote.

I tossed a pebble into the lake. The ripples it created became hundreds of self-replicating rhombuses, each containing an eyeball. The lake stared back at me, a thousand twinkling eyes. Then just as suddenly it morphed into a shimmering canvas of psychedelic yellows, greens, and blues. "To notice/The all/In the One," I wrote. Then I reprimanded myself for even thinking that I could describe so transcendent a scene: "Don't reflect. Look and see, observe and discover."

I sound so naive in my journal entry from that day. But that's who I was—a child of the sixties. And at a certain point, after encountering dragonflies that looked like angels and Amish farmers who all had the same face, I began to freak out. I felt myself separating from my body. Then I was floating toward heaven. From way up high I could see Matt and Kirk huddled around my coffin.

It was one of the scariest moments of my life. I felt as though the two sides of Abraxas, the light and the dark, were fighting a war for my soul. I somehow managed to put on an album that Matt had brought by tenor saxophonist John Coltrane, one of his favorite musicians. Coltrane and drummer Elvin Jones seemed to understand exactly what I was feeling. "Coltrane's sax is taking me to heaven: Louder, louder. Higher, higher," I wrote. "But the beat of Elvin's drums—steady, hard, constant—keeps me sane." In the background, pianist McCoy Tyner and bass player Jimmy Garrison chanted, "A Love Supreme. A Love Supreme. A Love Supreme." I began to calm down.

Coltrane's music described God and the experience of oneness with God better than anything I had ever read: A Love Supreme. His deeply felt "thank-you to God," as he called it, reawakened my own. "Yesterday I would have said that God is dead or has never been," I wrote in my journal. "But I have since sensed God's presence in a leaf, a lake, a meadow and a piece of music. When you add everything up—or take everything away—you get God."

Whatever had just happened had been one of the most powerful experiences in my life. My one and only LSD trip ended with a tearful, pulsating conviction that I would keep evolving toward a higher state of consciousness with my fellow travelers Kirk and Matt, and that I would continue to seek a sense of oneness with the universe.

But it wasn't meant to be.

Three days after we took acid, we reported on our TM experiences to the faculty of University School. All I remember about the session is how badly it went. The faculty agreed that it would be the last time any students at the school meditated for credit.

I SAW MATT only once that summer—out at his family's farm in the country. We talked about how deeply the acid trip had affected us, and how hard it would be to explain what happened that day to anyone else. Both of us had been unnerved by the experience. Like Demian's more convention-bound friends, I continued to be worried that I had done something terribly wrong, that I had opened a Pandora's box of emotions and perceptions that would haunt me for the rest of my life. I declared that I would never take acid again. Matt made no such promise. But his compassionate look said, "I understand what you are feeling."

Matt suggested that we go swimming at a nearby pond. The water cooled my skin. Then he climbed a tree and invited me to join him. I had followed my friend on a journey that had led me closer than I had ever been to experiencing God. But the idea of diving off that branch terrified me. So I stayed earthbound as he stretched out his arms and dove.

A few seconds later, he emerged from the water. Most teenage boys would have raised their arms in triumph. That wasn't Matt's style. He smiled gently, as if he were slightly embarrassed by his brave and graceful plunge.

THAT WAS THE summer of 1971. Matt went to Princeton and I went to Yale. For whatever reasons we didn't keep in touch. A few years later I realized that Matt's name was not listed in the University School alumni directory. I didn't attend our fifth high school reunion because I was traveling through Asia at the time. But at our tenth reunion, I asked Kirk if he knew what had happened to our good friend Matt. He said that Matt had changed his name, cut off ties with everyone from his past, and become a monk. That's why his name wasn't in the directory. He had requested that it never appear there again.

From time to time over the years, I wondered about Matt, both how he was doing and the choice he had made to cut himself off so completely from his past. But it wasn't until my year of taking care of unfinished business that I tried to find him. I contacted Kirk, who told me that Auxentios, the name Matt took when he became a monk, was a bishop in the Old Calendar Orthodox Church of Greece, and that he had founded a monastery in northern California with his spiritual father, Archbishop Chrysostomos, a well-known scholar.

From what I could piece together, Matt had studied at Princeton with Chrysostomos and with the late Georges Florovsky, perhaps the preeminent theologian of Orthodox Christianity in the world. Matt had been raised an Episcopalian, but he converted to Greek Orthodox during his junior year in college. Both he and Chrysostomos earned doctorates in theology from the Graduate Theological Union at Berkeley, and founded three monasteries together, including the one in California. Auxentios directed the Center for Traditionalist Orthodox Studies, where he edited a bimonthly periodical called *Orthodox Tradition* and books that were sold around the world.

Chrysostomos, who taught psychology when Matt was at Princeton, had accumulated a trunkful of degrees, including a Ph.D. from Princeton and fellowships to the Harvard Divinity School, Oxford University, and the U.S. Library of Congress. The archbishop was fluent in seven languages, and he had written more than fifty scholarly articles and a dozen books. His latest project was the first English translation ever of *The Evergetinos*, a book containing the sayings and wisdom of the Desert Fathers, the earliest Christian monks, who populated the desert regions of Egypt and Syria in the third and fourth centuries and practiced a rigorous asceticism that aimed to bring them closer to God.

The more I read about Chrysostomos and Auxentios, the less I knew what to think. On the one hand, I admired their efforts to preserve the practices and wisdom of the earliest Christians, and was fascinated by their asceticism, so contrary to our own times. But the stance the Old Calendarists took against interfaith dialogue bothered me. Without talking, how could people of different faiths even hope to get along?

In high school, Matt had been one of my most open-minded and curious friends. He could talk for hours about the intricacies of a butterfly wing or the beauty of a logarithm. He was genuinely interested in all of the world's religions, including Hinduism and Buddhism. But in his official photograph, he looked like Rasputin, the mad Russian mystic. Had he become a closed-minded fundamentalist, fighting a holier-than-thou war against progress?

I did what Kirk had advised and read *The Way of a Pilgrim*, the book that had inspired Matt to become Auxentios. In this first-person account, a barely literate peasant sets off over the steppes of Russia to learn how to "pray constantly," as the apostle Paul had instructed in his First Letter to the Thessalonians. Along the way, he reads the Philokia, a collection of writings by the Desert Fathers, and meets other Orthodox Christians, who deepen his understanding of prayer.

By the end of his journey, the pilgrim has learned to say the Jesus Prayer—"Lord Jesus Christ, Son of God, have mercy on me, a sinner"—in such a way that the prayer comes not from his lips or mind but from his heart. Father Jarvis had told me that prayer was an offering up to God of the mess we're in. The Jesus Prayer seemed more selfless and also mystical to me. It reminded me, in its use of repetition and breath to achieve inner stillness, of the techniques we had learned during our TM class. But instead of focusing on a mantra, a word empty of meaning, the Jesus Prayer invoked God and addressed Lord Jesus Christ directly.

Like the pilgrim in this beautiful story, I had been yearning for a connection to something larger, maybe even God. That feeling had been subtle, in the background of my life, for a long time. But when I saw Father Jarvis, it moved to the forefront again. I saw how Tony's spiritual life strengthened his ability to act selflessly and with compassion. It gave him the discipline and stamina he needed to do what I aspired to do: the right things. Auxentios, the ascetic, seemed even more pure in his pursuit of God. I wanted to see what that meant in terms of his everyday life. Was there any perspective he could offer me as I endeavored to complete the unfinished business of my life?

My fears that I would find no common ground with the bishop eased when I read an essay he had written in defense of Harry Potter. Orthodox reviewers had criticized the book series as being anti-Christian, a perspective that worried Auxentios. In defending the book, he warned his fellow Orthodox against becoming xenophobes and naysayers who couldn't see the good that science, medicine, and globalization was bringing the world. Harry Potter got kids to read and that was a good thing, he wrote. Behind that forbidding beard was a man who was much more tolerant than he looked.

I wrote Auxentios a letter thanking him for the role he had

played in awakening my spiritual side in high school. I told him how much I would like to see him again. He couldn't have been more generous and enthusiastic in his response. He invited me to visit the monastery in December, after he and the archbishop returned from a trip to Greece.

THE FLIGHT FROM San Francisco to Medford passed by snow-capped Mt. Shasta in Northern California and the Klamath National Forest in southern Oregon. En route, I tried to put the encounter I was about to have into perspective.

When I last saw him, in our teens, Matt and I were on a similar path. Then our paths diverged. Matt made a commitment to God and became a monk; I traveled through the Middle East and Asia until I was broke and became a bartender.

Until I was in my midthirties, my life was distinguished by my inability to stay committed to a job or a girlfriend; in wedding himself to God, Auxentios had maintained his vows of celibacy, obedience, and poverty.

By the age of forty, I was starting to build a family and career and, like my father before me, I had become an unrepentant worka-holic; Auxentios, now a bishop, had just finished building a monas-tery in Northern California, where he and his spiritual father trained other monks to carry on the traditions of the Desert Fathers.

In my midfifties, I wanted to pay more attention to my spiritual life in the hope that it would help me achieve a healthier balance between work and my relationships, and also because it would strengthen my resolve to live as fully as I could. And how about Auxentios? How well had the ascetic life served him? Was he happy in his life, did he long for anything, had he found peace?

The plane landed. By far the tallest person in the airport's wait-ing area waved to me as I walked through the gates. It was Auxen-tios, flanked by the archbishop and two nuns.

"Hello, Lee. We're so happy you arrived safely," Auxentios said. "This is His Eminence, Archbishop Chrysostomos, and Mothers Elizabeth and Catherine." The archbishop extended his hand and the mothers smiled, relieved that I had gotten to Medford without incident. "It will take us two hours to drive back to the monastery. Are you hungry, Lee?" Auxentios asked.

"I'm just happy to be here," I said.

Mother Elizabeth left the terminal to get the car. She returned several minutes later in a black SUV that looked brand-new. Auxentios helped the archbishop get into the front seat. But by the time he was able to help her squeeze into the third row of seats, Mother Catherine, an ample woman in her forties, had become wedged in the narrow space between the side door and second row of seats.

The bishop pushed then jostled her, then pulled every lever he could find, until the seat finally gave way. "This is our first trip in the car," Auxentios explained. "We are still getting used to it."

Their previous vehicle, a 1973 Mitsubishi van with over 250,000 miles on it, kept breaking down. When a wealthy parishioner told the monks that he wanted to buy them a car that actually ran, His Eminence concluded that the gift was justifiable and he gave the bishop permission to accept it. "We're very grateful, of course. I'll show you the old van when we pass through the town," Auxentios said. "With God's help, it served us well."

Travel was very much on Auxentios's mind this day. "It's getting harder for His Eminence to get around," he told me. "And I try to keep him comfortable." The two monks had just returned from their annual trip to Europe. Because His Eminence had emphysema and heart disease, he could no longer fly. So they took trains from Nevada to New York, a cruise ship to Paris, and more trains to Bulgaria, Romania, Athens, and Istanbul, visiting other church leaders along the way.

All of this talk must have made the archbishop hungry—or should I say hungrier—for he requested that we stop and have dinner at his favorite Chinese restaurant. This was clearly a treat for the arch-bishop, who had warned me about the mush that passed as food at the monastery. "You'll like the food here very much," he assured me. "We're vegetarian but please feel free to order anything you'd like."

I ordered exactly what everyone else did: sautéed tofu and vege-tables with fried rice. "You are probably thirsty from your trip," Chrysostomos said. "Why don't you order a beer?" I did, and so did the bishop, who requested a second glass so he could share it with His Eminence.

Late at night in a Chinese restaurant on the outskirts of Med-ford, Oregon, I settled into the company of two monks and two nuns, feeling out of place but happy. We sipped beer and listened to tales about the fourth-century early Christian monks and the Ess-enes, the Jewish monastic community that lived near the Dead Sea. I had expected Auxentios and Chrysostomos to be rigid and judg-mental, but they were good companions—and so were the moth-ers. The nuns and particularly Auxentios treated the archbishop with a tenderness I had seldom encountered, and it was touching. Although we made a strange group, I felt as relaxed and as joyful as I had felt in months.

Before we left, Chrysostomos pulled me aside and said, "His Grace will never tell you this. But I think you should know that eight years ago he was diagnosed with lymphoma. It was in his nasal passages, and it was very bad. His doctor gave him only two years to live."

It saddened me to think that my friend had suffered so much.

"He is cancer-free—our thanks be to God—but I want you to know that he handled his cancer with utmost dignity, never once grumbling about the chemotherapy or his pain. His only concern was for the brothers at the monastery, that they wouldn't worry about him and get distracted from their obediences and prayer."

"I'm not surprised," I told the archbishop. "Even in high school, he hated to draw attention to himself."

"No doubt His Grace would have been a model of humility, even if he had never been tonsured as a monk," the archbishop said. "If only I could become half as humble as His Grace, I would leave this world smiling."

AS WE DROVE on, we saw Mt. Shasta, all 14,179 feet of it, rising above the clouds. Auxentios unleashed a torrent of information about Mt. Shasta: "The name could have come from *chistly*, which is Russian for 'pure,' or it could have come from 'Susti'ka,' the name of a nearby tribe. It's a volcano, though dormant now. It erupted last in 1786 and will probably erupt again in the year 2500 or so." As Auxentios continued to regale us with obscure information about the mountain, I was reminded that he had been what my kids call a nerd in high school.

At the city limits, we came upon the famous Mitsubishi van. It looked every bit as run-down as Auxentios had said, only worse. A sign welcoming us to the town said that 790 people lived here. "That includes fourteen nuns, eleven monks, and seventy-three tonsured sheep," His Eminence teased.

A little before midnight we pulled into the monastery. Lit by the moon, it looked like a tiny Greek village, quietly beckoning us in the freshly fallen snow. I could see black shapes moving toward the SUV. One monk opened the door to help the archbishop out; another whispered something in the bishop's ear. Others moved quickly toward His Eminence and His Grace to kiss their hands. "Where's Svenski?" the archbishop asked, and a monk handed him his tiny white dog. "The brothers would like to welcome you," the bishop told me. And he led me through the snow toward the chapel.

BEFORE I WENT to sleep that night, I e-mailed Elizabeth about everything that had happened that day. What I had found most intriguing was Auxentios's relationship with his spiritual father: how he focused his full attention on Chrysostomos's safety and comfort, how he deferred to His Eminence before talking, how he attributed any wisdom or opinions he had to Chrysostomos. The other monks at the monastery treated Auxentios the same way in what I took to be a hierarchy of obedience and respect that rose upward toward God. It was fascinating to see how Auxentios so dutifully and even joyfully surrendered himself and his will to Chrysostomos and to Christ.

I knew that Elizabeth would frown upon the idea of a person cutting himself off from his parents and family in order to devote himself to a spiritual father or God. But for someone like Matt who wanted to dedicate himself fully to the religious life, I was beginning to understand the rationale. Christ was quoted as saying, "If any man come to me, and not hate his father and mother, wife and children and brethren and sisters, yea and his own life also, he cannot be my disciple." To be a true follower of Christ, you needed to be totally devoted to him, which meant renouncing your allegiances to your family, friends, and former self. That's why Matt had taken on the Christian name of Auxentios and become obedient to Chrysostomos, whose role was to guide him through the thicket of doubt and temptation that would challenge him.

You did not need to be celibate to be a good Christian, but Christ encouraged men who could accept it to make themselves "eunuchs for the kingdom of heaven's sake." Even here I was beginning to see the logic: If you were really set on purifying yourself and attaining an intimate knowledge of God, why complicate your already daunting task with the temptations and allures of physical love? The path that Matt had chosen for his spiritual growth was extraordinarily difficult, requiring the highest order of discipline and humility. But if he stayed true to that path, he could go to places I could never go.

* * *

THE FIRST PERCUSSIVE rat-a-tat-tat sounded at six A.M., waking the monks up. Thirty minutes later, there was another rat-a-tat-tat, followed by three clangs of a bell. Peering out of the curtains, I saw a dozen black shapes moving single file in the snow. I put on my coat and joined them as they walked to the chapel.

For the next hour, I watched what appeared to be a slow, somber, beautifully choreographed dance, as the monks moved from station to station and prayed. I had no idea what was going on. But the incense and chanting took my breath away.

After matins ended, a monk named Father Gregory gave me a tour. "The chapel is the center of our spiritual life," he told me. "And like our spiritual life, it is a work in progress," he said, pointing to one of the few areas still under construction.

The ceiling and walls were decorated with traditional icons depicting highlights from the Life of Christ, including the Transfiguration, Mystical Supper (as the Orthodox called it), Resurrection, Ascension, and Final Judgment. There were more icons of the Desert Fathers and the monastery's patron saints.

Even in the dim light, there was something bright and hopeful about these icons. The faces were elongated, and the scenes were rendered in shimmering red, orange, blue, green, and gold. I asked Father Gregory why the imagery was so idealized.

Quoting St. Anthony, Father Gregory said, " 'Christ became a man so that men could become God.' In everything we do we strive to cleanse and purify our minds so that we can grow closer to God. But our senses are too clouded by sin to perceive God's essence. So the icons function as 'windows into heaven.' They show things not as they appear but as they are transfigured by God's uncreated light and power."

Father Gregory told me how the monks prayed several times a day in the chapel. They also prayed while eating and working and when they were alone in their cells. What had led Father Gregory to this life of ceaseless prayer?

"When I turned eighteen, I decided to take responsibility for my own religious life," he told me. "I was raised Presbyterian, but I didn't know any other religion. So I read everything I could about the other Protestant denominations and about Hinduism, Buddhism, and Catholicism. My goal was to find the truest faith, by which I meant the one that was practiced by the people who had been closest to Jesus. And my research led me to Eastern Orthodoxy and to the early Christian monks who lived in the deserts of Egypt, Palestine, and Syria."

I asked the same question of Father John, the monk who brought my breakfast that morning. "Why did you become a monk?"

"I was born and raised a Catholic," Father John told me. "After high school I joined the navy and learned how to fix boilers. When I got out, I got a job fixing boilers at a power plant. I worked there for five years. The money was good, but then I started asking myself if there wasn't more to life than fixing boilers and paying the rent." Because he wasn't comfortable with the idea of papal infallibility— "I just don't believe that any human being is never wrong"—Father John began familiarizing himself with other religions. "One thing led to another and I found my way to Orthodoxy."

Father John had been at the monastery for nearly fourteen years. "At first, I was worried because I wasn't as educated as some of the other brothers," he said. "But, like the rest of the brothers, I have attached my fingers to the robes of the archbishop and the bishop, these really great men, with the hope that a little of their wisdom rubs off."

Father John left to check the boilers—his daily obedience. Another monk tended the monastery's two chickens and one goat. There was a monk who made wine and spirits from discarded blackberries, plums, and apples, and another whose obedience was to smoke and package the salmon that local fishermen donated from the surplus they caught at Klamath Falls.

The biggest "industry" at the monastery, though, was publishing.

Through the Center for Traditionalist Orthodox Studies, Bishop Auxentios published a quarterly magazine and several books a year. A number of the monks were involved, including one who ran the printing press. The center's most ambitious project was the archbishop's four-volume translation of *The Evergetinos*. His Eminence had begun translating this ancient text into English in the late 1980s when he was a research fellow at Oxford, and his goal now was to introduce the wisdom of the Desert Fathers to a new and younger audience in North America.

As soon as I got to my room, there was a knock at the door. It was Bishop Auxentios.

"Can we sit and talk now, Lee?" he asked.

"Of course," I answered.

Auxentios sat in the chair closest to the door—or rather, he draped himself over the chair. He was wearing a plain black cassock, a knit-wool hat and socks and sandals that covered his huge feet. He crossed his legs at his ankles, and while he talked, he propped his head on his left hand and stared down thoughtfully at his feet. Periodically he would look up. He said, "Thank you for visiting us, Lee. The brothers are pleased to have you here, and so is His Eminence."

"Everyone, especially you and the archbishop, has helped me feel very comfortable here," I said. "And I learned a lot on Father Gregory's tour."

"What have you noticed so far?" the bishop asked.

"For one thing, being a monk is a lot more demanding than I thought it would be. The brothers work and pray incredibly hard."

The bishop smiled. "How right you are in your observations about the brothers. Their sacrifices and dedication move and often shame me to tears."

"From talking with the brothers, I've gotten at least a small idea why some of them ended up here. Father Gregory was looking for the truest Christianity. And Father John was searching for something deeper and more lasting than a paycheck. They both expressed how lucky they feel to be in the presence of the archbishop and you."

"His Eminence is the spiritual father to all of us," Auxentios said, deflecting the brothers' praise.

"But in talking with them, I got to wondering about you. When you and I were in high school, we studied Hinduism and Buddhism together. I don't remember any strong inclination you had toward Christianity, much less Orthodox Christianity. What happened?"

The bishop looked quizzically at me, then down at his sandals. Then he gathered his thoughts.

"You are right," he finally said. "When we knew each other, I did not think of myself as being particularly Christian. My parents sent us to Bible school, but when I was really young, I would guess eight, we suddenly stopped going. I do not think my parents had any reason to quit the church beyond the fact they had a complicated life, with five sons. But it left me with a longing, Lee. That my longing became focused on Hinduism and Buddhism, I think it mostly had to do with the fact that my older brother Chris was reading the Bhagavad Gita and Hermann Hesse's *Siddhartha* at the time."

"When did Christianity enter the picture?" I asked. "And when did you decide to become a monk?"

Again, there was a long pause. I looked over the room. The suite we were sitting in had been built two years earlier in anticipation of a visit from the archbishop's spiritual father. Metropolitan Cyprian, who lived in Athens, was the most important figure in Old Calendar Orthodoxy, and his health at the time was declining. So the brothers worked for months to create a room that would be comfortable for him. The room was larger than most, a bedroom with separate bath, and for guests like me, there was an AM/FM radio, chocolate candies, and a bottle of the monastery's plum wine.

"Thinking back, I first considered becoming a monk during my freshman year at Princeton," the bishop said. "I had a relationship that did not turn out well, and I was feeling emotionally empty. So I bicycled from Cleveland to Colorado and spent several days in a Buddhist monastery. I told the head of the monastery that I wanted to become a monk, but he told me to go back to college. The same thing happened in New York City, when I visited a Zen monastery there. The roshi told me to finish school." He paused, this time for only a moment or two. "Spiritually, I was all over the place. If I had become a Buddhist monk, I would have done it for the wrong reasons."

During his sophomore year at Princeton, Matt took a course that Chrysostomos taught.

"His Eminence was a layman then, and it was a course in the psychology of personality. There was nothing special about our relationship. I was just another student, I think. But occasionally I would see him between classes in the Princeton quad, and we'd talk about religion. He knew that I was searching for something deeper, and one time he suggested that I visit Mount Athos in Greece. I filed the suggestion away, then forgot about it. But a year later, I took a train across Europe and, on a lark really, I sought and received permission from the Greek authorities to visit Athos."

Located on the Halkidiki Peninsula in Macedonia, Mount Athos is to Eastern Orthodoxy what Mecca is to Muslims, Varanasi is to Hindus and Jerusalem is to Jews—the religion's pulsating heart. More than fifteen hundred monks live in monasteries and sketes on Mount Athos and also alone in caves. It was here that St. Gregory Palamas learned how to achieve inner stillness and pray—and it was here that Matt discovered his calling.

"I knew, after spending several weeks in the monasteries of Mount Athos, that I would become an Orthodox Christian and a monk. When I got back to Princeton, I took a course from Father Florovsky, the esteemed Orthodox theologian. He and the archbishop—who was still a layman at the time—encouraged me to convert to Greek as opposed to Russian Orthodoxy because the Greek Old

Calendarists were more fervent in their beliefs. I began talking a great deal with the archbishop about what living a spiritual life would mean—the commitment and sacrifices I would need to make—and spent most of that year commuting to Princeton from a monastery on Long Island."

There was a knock on the door. It was Father John with a message from the archbishop. "His Eminence would like to see you in five minutes," he said. I followed Auxentios's lead and got up from my chair.

"Luckily, we don't have far to go," he said. The archbishop was waiting for us two doors away, in the Metropolitan Cyprian Sitting Room. The room was filled with photographs of the Metropolitan and other leading figures in the Old Calendar Orthodox Church of Greece.

"I was about to tell Lee about our first monastery—the one in San Bernadino—and how the pollution was damaging to your lungs," the bishop said. "After that, we moved to Hayesville, Ohio, and began building a monastery there."

That was the last time I would hear Auxentios's voice until I left the room half an hour later. It was as though he had teed up His Eminence to tell the rest of the story.

"We were destitute," His Eminence began. "So at night we worked in a diner. Imagine it. These two scruffy monks, their beards down to here, looking like Yeshiva U. grad students, the bishop cooking, yours truly waiting tables, in a Greek diner in the land of cows, corn bread, and Harleys."

BEFORE LUNCH I read a sermon that Archbishop Chrysostomos had given several years ago about the purpose of worship. In it, he described the meaning behind everything that I'd experienced that morning, and its contrast with more contemporary forms of worship.

He wrote:

The purpose of worship—the very voice of God in silence and with our minds and eyes darkened to the world, focused on the windows into the other world that are our icons, our senses saturated by incense, our egos humbly subdued in pious standing and prayer—has been thwarted. Today, having adopted Western ideas of worship, we scream and sing at God, making such a din that we do not hear Him speaking to us. How far we are from the experience of that small inner voice, through which God speaks to our hearts. Our participation should be silence, submission and awe before the splendor of God. And our prayers and chants should not be pronouncements before God, but supplications for God to speak to us and be with us.

I was beginning to see why Matt was so attracted to Orthodoxy: It offered a path toward enlightenment that was earned through the hard work of cleansing yourself of sin and living selflessly and in service to God. Because the ascetic path was littered with obstacles and pitfalls, because it required genuine sacrifice, because it tested you until you abandoned your pride and willfulness and lived only for God, it was a road he could trust.

During a brief moment in high school, and with the help of a drug, I had experienced the transcendence of my ego and the frightening beauty of a universe where I was no better or worse, no weaker or more powerful, than anyone or anything else. Then my ego was back and that feeling of oneness with the universe and God was gone. After high school, Matt became even more intense in his desire to experience God, following a path that required a life of struggle, denial, and inward-directed prayer. It was considerably more removed and mystical than the path Tony took.

My main goal, in seeing Tony and then Auxentios, was to get their perspectives on my intention to complete my unfinished business and lead a more balanced and purposeful life. It was clear, from observing their lives, that doing right took constant vigilance. It also took commitment and hard work. Where did God fit into the equation for me? I wasn't sure. But I did know that a spiritual dimension would be necessary if I were to redirect and move ahead with my life.

A LITTLE BEFORE six P.M., the monks were summoned to dinner. We walked silently and single file into a spare, white refectory that was adorned with icons of St. Gregory Palamas and Christ. There was a long table for the eleven monks and me, and a shorter one for the bishop and His Eminence.

Like everything at the monastery, the meal was modest—tofu mixed together with bits of celery and peppers. Throughout the meal, the monks ate in silence, with their eyes riveted on the center of their plates. Father Gregory stood at a lectern and read the accounts of several fifteenth-century Christian martyrs who had suffered horrible deaths after they refused to convert to Islam. When they were finished eating, the monks walked single file out of the refectory and back to their cells to pray. I had never had a quicker, more regimented, more instructional meal, and I was still hungry. Fortunately, Father John brought a tray of tea and cookies to my room. After arranging the tea on the table between the two chairs, he said, "His Grace will be by shortly," and left the room.

A few minutes later, there was another knock at the door. It was Bishop Auxentios, and I could tell, by the tilt of his head, that he was troubled. Was it something I had said to him in a previous conversation? Or something he had just thought? Perhaps he had caught himself yearning, like I had, for a second helping of food?

In everything I had read, monks were described as scientists of the soul, engaged in a lifelong experiment to see how close human beings could get to mirroring the perfection of God. The men who chose to be monks tended toward perfectionism, and being a perfectionist is never easy. You scrub your soul raw so that sin can't take root there, and then you scrub again. But how can you be sure that you've done everything in your power to keep evil and temptation at bay? You can't, of course, so you keep scrubbing. Perhaps I was seeing Auxentios in the process of cleansing himself of something that would have meant absolutely nothing to you or me.

Auxentios and the monks spent most of their time looking inward, and I could certainly see the value in that. As I set about completing my unfinished business, I saw how much I had let important things slide and friends fall by the wayside because I was so overly concerned with my work. My need to work was linked to my fears of failure and of not being able to provide for my family. Unless I confronted those fears by looking inward, I would keep on working compulsively at the expense of my larger life and relationships with people who mattered most to me.

If I was to truly change, I would need to look inward, as Matt had done. In his desire to cleanse himself of sin and pray constantly from the heart, Matt continued to direct his focus inward. But once I faced my fears, I knew my instinct would be to look outward again and direct my energies toward other people and the larger world. It was there that I had found the greatest rewards in my life, in the circle of compassion that I had experienced in the world of people, whether it was in my family, with Andre after his great loss, or with some of the social causes I'd worked on over time.

Did the monks, who were so inner directed, feel any compulsion to look to the outer world, feed the hungry, or care for the sick? Did they see a need to fight the evils outside themselves?

From the bishop's very considered pause, I could see that I had touched on a matter of fundamental principle. "Most people who lead a spiritual life believe that nothing is truly harmful, except what one can do to oneself," he said. "There is overwhelming testimony from observant, spiritual, and sanctified individuals that what I say is not based on theory, but on truth."

"What about the Nazi Holocaust?" I asked. "Or nuclear war? Isn't it our moral obligation to do everything in our power to prevent these evils from happening?"

"Not from the spiritual perspective, Lee. The way those of us who lead the spiritual life see it, people can get so easily disturbed by social, general, and universal evil that they ignore the evil inside themselves."

Bishop Auxentios closed his eyes. I could tell that he was trying to find a better way to explain what he meant to me.

"You see, ground zero for combating evil is the human heart," he said. "One helps the poor, rights the wrong, and contributes to the better functioning of society because the inner voice of conscience dictates these actions. I find social activism that is not accompanied by internal transformation troubling."

"So what about the millions of men, women, and children who will die in Darfur if we don't stand up to their oppressors?" I asked. "Aren't we complicit in their genocide?"

"Not according to the spiritual outlook," Auxentios said. "Victimization is often inescapable in this fallen world. For those who meet that fate with meekness, love, forgiveness, and even joy, I see ultimate triumph—victory for the so-called victim. The perpetrator is the real victim—of his passions and evil—and suffers the worst, eternal consequences."

You needed to believe in God, an afterlife, and a divinely ordained system of justice to accept Auxentios's outlook. If you were unsure of these things, as I was, it was hard to understand his spiritual perspective. But I tried. Was he telling me that persecution offered the hope of deification to its victims, in which case individuals and nations should never intervene? Or maybe I was missing his point. Perhaps he was simply saying, "Don't let other people's evil distract you from taking responsibility for your own."

"So," I ventured to Auxentios, "the most important fight we human beings wage is the battle within."

"Yes, Lee. As His Eminence always teaches: Our primary task is to correct the microcosm before tackling the macrocosm."

As the bishop said that, I understood what he meant when he said that he found "social activism without inner transformation troubling." He meant that a person's efforts to change the world should be dictated by "the inner voice of his conscience."

During the past several months, I had been going through an inner transformation that was enabling me to act with more compassion toward myself and the people who mattered to me. Although Auxentios and the monks were clearly at a level in their spiritual development that far exceeded anything I could even imagine, I did feel that I was in the process of purifying my heart and attuning myself to my conscience, from which my actions increasingly flowed. First, I needed to confront my fears. Once I had done that, I was able to reach out to other people. The third part of the process was to reflect on how that experience of reconnecting had affected both me and the person to whom I had reached out.

There was definitely a discipline to the process: Unless I faced my fears, I couldn't reach out beyond myself; unless I reached out, there was nothing to reflect upon; unless I reflected on what was happening, there was no growth or refinement of my conscience, so that my actions could keep flowing consistently from it. I wanted to share what I had just realized with the bishop, but before I could say anything, Father John peered inside the door and kissed his hand. "Are you finished with your tea?"

"Yes," the bishop said. "Will you please tell His Eminence that we will be joining him shortly, Father. His Eminence would like to spend more time with Lee before he leaves in the morning."

As we walked down the snowy path toward the archbishop's

cell, I asked Auxentios a question that had been on my mind for most of the day. "The way you describe it, spiritual growth is an all-consuming twenty-four-hour-a-day obedience that requires total focus and discipline. Does a person need to be a monk in order to achieve true spiritual growth?"

"I am sorry to have given you that impression, Lee," he said. "What I believe—and I think His Eminence would agree—is that each human being exists on a different level of spiritual growth. The brothers here strive to live the life of Christ in order to become united with God. But for some people, spiritual growth can come from something as seemingly small as overcoming a grudge. You need to determine your own level, then work from there." My own level was becoming clearer to me.

A TYPICAL MONK'S cell is only slightly wider than a cot, and contains a desk, a light, and a chair. But with his limited mobility—and his need to stay in touch with Orthodox communities around the world—the archbishop required a slightly wider cell. It was furnished with a leather reading chair, a flat-screen computer, a television set equipped with TIVO, and a big comfy pillow for Svenski, his very spoiled dog.

His Eminence had summoned me so that we could discuss current events. I could tell that he considered this a treat. As he had told me earlier in the day, "You have to overlook my frenzy. Intellectually, I am like a starving man at times. When someone comes by peddling noetic foie gras, I am out in the streets, fork in hand, wildly stabbing the air."

His Eminence had well-informed opinions about the war in Iraq ("a travesty"), the election of Barack Obama ("let's wait and see, with hope"), and the persistence of anti-Semitism among fringe elements of the Orthodox Church ("it saddens and amazes me on so many levels, particularly given the fact that the early Christian

monks were so deeply influenced by the first-century Jewish mo-
nastics, and the fact that so many Eastern Orthodox, including
several bishops I know, have Jewish blood").

Maybe twice a month, the monks got to watch a *Frontline* or
National Geographic special that had been vetted for sexually pro-
vocative content by the bishop. But on this, my final night at the
monastery, Auxentios and I got to watch the *NBC Nightly News
with Brian Williams* with the archbishop. His Eminence had also
recorded the latest episode of *Monk,* a show about a brilliant detec-
tive who is afflicted with obsessive-compulsive disorder. It was the
archbishop's favorite show, and we laughed at the irony of this
monk who was addicted to *Monk.*

His Eminence told several stories about a man he had deeply
admired: St. John of Shanghai and San Francisco, the Russian-
born monk who had ministered to the poor and built orphanages
for indigent children. St. John had predicted several events of consequence, including the hour of his own death.

And then it was time for me to head to my room and pack.

Before I left, the archbishop apologized for stumbling over his
words. "Living here takes its toll on one's vocabulary," he explained.
Then, with a comic's expert timing, he said, "except for those times
when one can wedge in a meaningful epithet between grunts, farts,
affirmations that Jeeesus and Joseph Smith save, and belches from
the last cow burger with greasy fries and really cheap beer." The
bishop and I laughed. "Sleep well," His Eminence said.

NEXT MORNING, I finished my packing and had breakfast in my
room. Then I had a final coffee with the bishop. Before I went back
to New York, he wanted to know if I knew anything about two
other friends of his from high school. He feared that one of them—
a classmate of ours—had died. ("I do not know why, Lee, but I have
an intuition about it.") He was happy to hear that this friend was

alive and well and living in Florida, but sad to learn that his other friend—an older boy, who had been a brilliant student and poet— had been institutionalized after a drug-induced nervous break- down.

Auxentios and I talked briefly about the day we took acid. The bishop's memory of that day was clouded, but he characterized himself during those years as being "ungrateful, misdirected, and heedless." I could tell that he felt conflicted about the past, which gave me an opening to ask about his relationship with his parents. He said he got along fine with them now. But for many years, after he first became tonsured as a monk, he kept his distance from them. He traced the rift to a time that his mother suggested that His Eminence was a svengali, bent on controlling his life, and Aux- entios felt betrayed.

"I was too stubborn and proud to forgive her," he said. As he spoke about his mother, whom I remembered as a kind and beautiful woman, he did so with affection. When he got ill with cancer, his parents came to the monastery several times a year to care for him. Their love softened his heart. His mother was making an effort to learn more about Orthodoxy, even though her memory, at age eighty- three, was failing. This too heartened him.

Most of us see ourselves as part of two stories—our personal nar- rative and the ongoing story of our family. Bishop Auxentios has only a passing interest in those stories. Instead, he views himself as part of a story that began nearly two thousand years ago in the des- erts of Egypt, Palestine, and Syria, and that continues today in the lives of the small numbers of men and women who use prayer, fast- ing, celibacy, and obedience to cleanse themselves of impurity and unite their hearts with God.

I got a taste of that life when I visited the bishop. And although I would never choose it for myself—I am way too in love with my wife and kids—I can appreciate those who do.

* * *

ON OUR WAY to the car, Auxentios and I picked up His Eminence
at his cell and walked through the courtyard, with its three lime-
stone sepulchers. Like any community that has survived for thirty
years, the monastery had begun to accumulate its own dead. Two
of the sepulchers contained the bodies of the first two monks who
had grown old and died from natural causes at the monastery. The
third sepulcher held the body of a local priest's son who had been
killed in a car accident in Greece.

Once the bodies decomposed, the bones would be placed in an ossuary, leaving room in the sepulchers for the next monks who die. But
because the brothers had been so busy with other obediences—
planting the vineyard, building the chicken coop, and finishing Metropolitan Cyprian's suite—the ossuary had yet to be built.

"It has moved to the top of our to-do list," the bishop told me as
we reached the brand-new SUV that would take me to the airport.
"We're hoping to build the ossuary by the end of the year."

"Not so fast," the archbishop said with a scowl. "Why are you
and the brothers so intent on burying me?"

The bishop leaned over and kissed the archbishop's hand. "Now
you see what's really holding us up," he laughed. "His Eminence is
nowhere near ready to repose."

There was, as always, a sweetness in the bishop's laugh, but there
was another quality, too. Many years ago I watched as my friend
Matt climbed to the top of a huge tree, then dove into a pond with
an angel's grace and the abandon of a fighter pilot. I envied his courage then, but it was his humility that awed me now. As suggested
by its root word, "humus," which means soil, the truly humble view
themselves as no better than anyone else, including the earth they
walk on. Auxentios was truly humble. I could never approach him
in quiet virtue or prayerful obedience, but for inspiration, I would
always look his way.

*   *   *

THE RED-EYE FROM Medford to New York landed at six in the morning. I was home by nine.

I had been fearful of disturbing Auxentios's life and serenity when I visited him. But just as I had misread Andre and my aunt Fern, I had underestimated his ability to deal with the past. By the time I got home, he had sent me the following e-mail: "Our time together refreshed not only the memory of some of our words and deeds but, more importantly, some well-intentioned aspirations." He added that "like all beneficial experiences in spiritual life," my visit had left him "all the more motivated and enthused" about his decision to become a monk.

Later that day, Elizabeth and I hosted our annual Chanukah party. Each year, we invite sixty or so of our friends to our cramped apartment and feed them brisket and the traditional potato pancakes called latkes. This year's party made me especially happy. I had enjoyed my visit to the monastery, but I knew that whatever spiritual progress I made in my life, it would happen right here, with the people in this room.

Only a small number of people are called to be monks; the rest of us are meant to be citizens of our communities, nations, and planet, and to lead our spiritual lives while fulfilling our duties as sons and daughters, fathers and mothers, husbands and wives, and neighbors. Outside of the monastery's walls, the temptation to lie, cheat, steal, take shortcuts, become lazy, zone out, turn a deaf ear, covet everything in sight, and eat everything on everybody else's plate is huge. So is the temptation to think only about ourselves. But none of us is perfect. And that's why Auxentios's theory of different spiritual levels is so encouraging. For some people, spiritual growth means sitting at the top of a pole and fasting for thirty days. But for others, it means surmounting the pettiness that keeps us mad at our parents, lovers, or bosses, or reaching out to a stranger in need.

What's important is that we register whatever spiritual progress we make inside ourselves so that we can continue to evolve. His Eminence would say that we are meant to be gods by virtue of the fact that God became a man. I don't challenge that formulation, but because I'm Jewish, I don't embrace it either. Here's what I do know: In the hurly-burly life we lead, with its constant barrage of distractions, it is important to take our soul's measure in a quiet place, and frequently.

We need to ask ourselves: Am I allowing myself enough quiet and stillness in my life so that I can hear "the small inner voice, through which God speaks to our hearts"?

My own level of spiritual development is becoming clearer and clearer to me. To grow spiritually, I need to become a more loving, kind, giving, and thankful person to the people around me, particularly Elizabeth and the kids. If I put down my work when Caroline has something important to tell me, or if I can hold Noah when he is sad instead of turning away, I will have advanced a huge rung on my ladder of spiritual growth. And I can thank my friend the bishop for helping me to realize this.

At the beginning of this chapter, I resolved to find a friend who took the road less traveled. For each of us, the road less traveled may be different. If you are a lawyer or businessman, it may be the road that would have led you to become a poet or musician. If you are a woman who pursued a career, it may have been the one that led to your staying home to raise your kids. There are some roads that only a handful of people follow—such as circus clown or demolitionist. And others that many people travel, but not you. So consider seeking out a friend who shared your dreams when you were young but went off in a totally different direction. See where his life took him and where it might have taken you. At the very least, the two of you will share photos and memories. Or you may gain new insights into yourself and your future and take the measure of your soul.

CHAPTER EIGHT

The Day Eliot Ness Set My
Grandfather Straight—
Or Did He?

Healing a Family's Wounds

IT HAD BEEN wonderful to see Pudge open his heart to Fern and
visit her, but the gulf between my uncle and father remained as
wide as ever, causing their wives and children considerable pain.
Was there anything I could do to help them mend their relationship before it was too late?

As I pursued my own unfinished business, I had seen glimmers of
a possible relationship between the two brothers. When Pudge told
me how pleased he had been to visit Fern, I was encouraged to ask if
he'd like to see Harry again. He didn't answer me at the time, but I
had planted a seed. When I started coaching Ben, I was surprised to
see how tolerant I had become of my father's heavy-handed sayings
and advice. If I could help Pudge and Harry reconcile, I sensed that
my own relationship with my father would continue to improve.

If I had learned anything on my journeys to complete my unfinished business, it was that reaching out transforms you. Every time
I extended myself to someone else, something good happened—
and I became a happier person. But helping my father and his brother
reconcile would be tricky. In 1990, Pudge's oldest son and one of my
brothers had arranged a surprise meeting between the two men on a
Chicago street corner. It lasted five awkward minutes. The brothers
retreated to their respective cabs and never spoke of the encounter,
or to each other, again. If I was to succeed where that attempt had
failed, I would need to approach them separately, and indirectly,
and get them together in a way that wouldn't threaten or alienate
them.

I kept coming back to the idea that nothing excites the men in my family more than a good mob story. Get them talking about the old days of our family's rubber-and-tire business and they would soon be at each other's throats, full of blame and acrimony. But if you mentioned any of the union or mob bosses they knew, they'd launch into their stories with relish, recounting their every encounter with Mo, Maishe, Bones, and Jackie. If I got Pudge and Harry involved in a good mob story, I might be able to break the ice. Fortunately, I had one. It was a story my grandmother told me dozens of times when I was young:

> During Prohibition your grandfather and his brothers made a small fortune selling corn sugar to bootleggers. Believe me, Lee Richard, this was a dangerous business, they could have been killed.
>
> The Kravitzes competed with the two big Italian mob families—the Porrellos and the Lonardos. On the night the Porrello brothers were murdered, Eliot Ness himself, the greatest crime fighter of all time, showed up at your great-grandfather's grocery store. I'm not kidding, Lee Richard, I was there. He was such a good-looking young man. He asked to see your grandfather. He said, "I like you, Benny. You're a nice kid." Then he told him, "Get out of this business, Benny." And Benny did.

Had it taken place in Chicago and not Cleveland, this famous family story could have been a scene from *The Untouchables,* the movie that pitted so-called G-man Eliot Ness against crime boss Al Capone. A boyish Kevin Costner would have played Ness, just as he did in the movie. And a short, chunky, balding actor would have played my grandpa Benny.

I had repeated the Ness story dozens of times—to women I wanted to impress, to my children for a better-than-usual bedtime story, and to myself as an explanation for how my family had achieved the riches it later lost.

But, over the years, I had also wondered whether the story was true. Had Eliot Ness set my grandfather straight and kept him from a life of crime? While I had my job, I could never free up the time it would take to authenticate the story. But now I could—and I could take my father and uncle along for the ride. They would be essential sources.

I decided to subject the Ness story to the same rigor I would apply to any story I was editing for a magazine. I would pore over newspaper articles and court records; verify times, dates, and locations; ensure the accuracy of all quotes and probe any detail that seemed suspect or out of place.

Because everyone who had witnessed or appeared in my grandmother's story was dead, I would need to rely on second- and third-hand accounts of friends and relatives of Ness, the Porrellos, and my grandparents. That would give me an opening to talk with all of the Kravitzes who weren't talking with each other, including my father and Pudge. The first thing I would need to do was check whether the story I had heard from Nana Shirley was the one she had told everyone else.

I e-mailed it to my father. "Is this the story she told *you?*"

"Close enough," he wrote back. Ever since my grandparents died, my father has prided himself on being the family historian. "Nobody alive knows more than me. Pudge, the rest, they'll tell you things . . . But they weren't there. I'M THE ONLY ONE WHO ACTUALLY LIVED ABOVE CHATZA'S GROCERY STORE . . . UNTIL I WAS 4 YEARS OLD. Like Edward R. Murrow, 'I WAS THERE.'"

What interested my father even more than Ness was a mob story that involved him. In 1932 or 1933, when he was an infant, the Lonardo crime family allegedly kidnapped my dad. "They wanted the Kravitzes to sell them more corn sugar," he explained. "SO THEY

SENT YOUR GRANDPA BENNY A MESSAGE. They drove me 'around the block' a few times, then 'dropped me back' on the DOORSTEP."

When I visited my uncle Pudge in Los Angeles, he neither confirmed nor denied the kidnapping story and claimed that he couldn't contribute anything more than his brother had to the Ness saga. "Look, I'm five years younger than Harry, and by the time I was old enough to remember anything, my parents were off doing their own thing, building the business and all, and I was an after-thought."

Pudge still seemed peeved by that slight. "Harry was the prince. That's just the way it was. I don't hate your father," he said. "I just never liked him." And now, at age seventy-two, Pudge said he felt no special urge to reconcile with my father. "Life's short," he explained. "You make your priorities."

"Do you want me to keep you posted if I find out anything more about Ness?" I asked.

"Yeah, sure," he said.

I took this to be a positive sign. For more than two decades, Harry had been absent from my conversations with Pudge, and Pudge had been missing from my letters from Harry. But now, at the beginning of my hunt for the truth about Ness, the disenfranchised brothers had at least uttered each other's names. And they both wanted to be kept in the loop. This meant that I could copy them on the same e-mails. Tiny as it was, I considered it a breakthrough.

AS I STARTED to involve my father and uncle in fact-checking the Ness story, I remembered something Tony Jarvis had told me: "Love takes work. It demands that you put yourself in the shoes of another person—and understand where that person is coming from—before you speak or act."

For most of my life, I had not put myself in my father's shoes as he went about the rough-and-tumble business of providing for his family and fathering his children. Whether I was on the receiving end of his sage advice about how life should be lived or of the hectoring instructions to throw the Big One from the mound, I'd found his style hard to take and often reeled away. His reluctance to reach out to his brother Pudge was all part of the pattern. Often I simply treated him as if he were a shallow, narrow-minded child. It perplexed me that he couldn't see how emotionally damaging his childish grudges were, how destructive his hard and fast opinions could be. Didn't he see the pain his feuds were causing his sons and his wife; didn't he see that he was constantly throwing up walls that kept everyone at a distance?

And yet, this was the man who wrote to me religiously every week for years on end, the evidence of which I had now safely stored in a new, specially dedicated cardboard box. And here also was the man who took evident, almost embarrassing pride in his family and considered himself the family historian. Lately, as I had started addressing my own unfinished business, I began to see my father through a more compassionate lens, as someone who was experiencing his own deep pain. He had been completely deaf for more than twenty years, had had to deal with a major career crisis in midlife, and had not had a job in ten years. His life in many ways had been hard, but he had accepted it without complaint.

What bothered my father, I think, was the way the world was changing. It was changing fast—it had always changed fast—and it made him unsure of himself and of his role in it. When he was growing up, the family business was solid and growing and something you could count on; that had all changed. At the time he had lived in the home of his grandparents Chatza and Rochel, children revered their elders; now they ignored them. At age seventy-seven, my father had outlived every male in the history of the Kravitz family. But his children lived all over the country, in four different cities, and didn't keep in touch.

I was beginning to reach out to him, and as I did, I was starting to understand his perspective better. My father, despite his deafness, despite his setbacks, had achieved a lot over the years. He had worked until his midsixties; he had sent all four sons to college; he had taught hundreds of young boys to love baseball and learn good values from the sport. He was a proud man facing an unsure world, and you don't just tell a man like my father what to do or how to behave. You let him come to his own conclusions, embrace a change on his own terms.

In the past months I felt that my father and I had lessened the distance between us, and I wanted that to continue. I hoped that in trying to bring him and his brother Pudge together I would be able to kill two birds with one stone.

My fact-checking strategy would take time and work, and there would be absolutely no guarantee of success. As Tony warned, "Love of this sort can be inconvenient, unpleasant, costly." I bought a plane ticket to Cleveland to see another relative who might shed light on the mystery of Ness—my father's younger and equally estranged cousin, Harley.

WHEN I ARRIVED at Harley's country club, the hostess led me to a table that overlooked one of the most manicured golf courses in America. In 1996, Tom Watson had won the U.S. Open on this course.

"Mr. Kravitz is our club's president," she said.

"I didn't know that," I lied.

"And he's one of our best golfers."

Harley got up and gave me a big bear hug. He was short and stocky like the rest of us and cocked his head a bit to the right when he smiled.

"Alice is making me sound a lot better than I really am," he said. "I'm at six. My dad used to be a two-handicap golfer."

Harley's dad, my uncle Oscar, was Ben's younger brother. Years before he died, he was incapacitated by a massive stroke, which was how I remembered him. I wondered whether Oscar had ever said anything to Harley about Eliot Ness.

"You bet he did," Harley said. "He told me a hell of a story about the time Ness showed up at your great-grandfather's store with his Untouchables. Chatza—he was a tough son of a bitch—wouldn't let them in. So Ness pushed Chatza to the side and called for Ben, who lived above the store."

"Was Shirley there?" I asked, knowing that my grandmother would play as little a role in Oscar's version as Oscar had played in hers.

"Not to my knowledge," Harley answered. "Only Oscar, Ben, and Chatza. Dad told me that Ness showed them files of receipts from the suppliers who had sold them corn sugar. The Kravitzes had been buying a ton of corn sugar, and Ness wanted to know where it went. Ben and my dad couldn't produce any receipts, so Ness knew they'd been selling their corn sugar to bootleggers. He said, 'Get out now and I'll leave you alone.'

"Dad said Ben convinced Ness to give them the weekend so they could settle their affairs. Your grandpa had chutzpah. He really did. The Kravitzes made a fortune that weekend."

For the most part, the story that Oscar had told Harley was consistent with the story my grandmother had told me. But Harley told me something else about Ness's relationship with the Kravitzes that I had never heard.

"It was after the war," he said. "Ness was out of work and drinking too much and came to Ben and Oscar for help. They gave him a job selling motor mounts. It was part-time, on commission I think. The arrangement lasted for years, until Ness died."

I couldn't believe it. Broke, depressed, and addicted to booze—this was not the church-boy G-man played by Robert Stack. Could my grandfather really have given him his dignity back?

But first things first.

MY GRANDMOTHER'S STORY hinged on a single fact: that Ness visited Chatza's store on the same day the Porrellos were murdered. If I could prove that Ness was in Cleveland on the day the Porrellos were killed, then her story would be more believable, giving Pudge, Harry, and Harley a common ground on which to agree.

My research led me to the Western Reserve Historical Society. Offhand, the librarian didn't know the date of the Porrello murders or whether Ness was in town that day. But she gave me a number of books and newspaper articles that chronicled the activities of mobsters and bootleggers in Cleveland during the 1920s and '30s, when the Eighteenth Amendment produced a vast underground economy of stills and speakeasies in the city.

Zucchero di grano, or corn sugar, fueled that economy. A little less than six pounds of corn sugar could make a gallon of whiskey, and grocery store owners like my great-grandfather Chatza had access to a ready supply.

But the real money went to the Lonardo and Porrello families, who used bribes and intimidation to build competing empires. Between 1920 and the end of Prohibition, more than one hundred people were murdered in Cleveland's bloody corn sugar wars. The worst of the violence began on December 11, 1927, when "Big Joe" Lonardo and his brother John were shot to death in the back of Ottavio Porrello's barbershop. Soon bodies started showing up in lakes, ravines, and the trunks of abandoned cars.

On July 5, 1930, Ottavio's brother Joe was gunned down in a saloon in the Little Italy section of Cleveland. According to the *Cleveland News,* "At 2:27, Joe Porrello fell with three bullets in his head. Hung between his lips was a cigarette, freshly lighted." Three weeks later, Joe's brother Jim was murdered as he shopped for groceries. "He fell while ordering lamb chops at the meat counter," reported the *News*.

The killings continued until February 25, 1932, when Raymond and Rosario Porrello were shot to death as they played blackjack in the back of a cigar store they owned at East 110th Street and Woodland Avenue, three blocks away from Chatza's store.

My research was nearly done. The Porrellos were killed on three separate days: July 5, 1930; July 26, 1930; and February 25, 1932. Now I needed to find out whether Ness was anywhere near Chatza's store on one of those days. From the news clippings, I put together a chronology: Until the end of Prohibition, in 1933, Ness worked in Chicago as a special investigator for the Justice and Treasury Departments. Then he worked in Cincinnati for a year for the government's Alcohol Tax Unit. It wasn't until August 16, 1934, that he set foot in Cleveland as ATU's investigator at large for northern Ohio. By then the five Porrellos were dead and my grandfather had already begun his rubber-and-tire company.

I HAD BEGUN fact-checking the Ness story because I needed a tool that could help me mend the rift that existed between my uncle and my father. Like the other Kravitzes of their generation, Harry and Pudge could spend hours talking about the mobsters they had known. The Ness story had the makings of a perfect icebreaker.

I also had a less tactical reason for fact-checking Ness: I wanted to keep my grandpa Benny alive for as long as I could. The people who had known my grandfather in his glory years—when he started his company and devoted his life to helping others—were nearly all dead. In fact-checking Ness, I could learn more details about my grandfather's life, which I could pass on to my children and grandchildren, keeping him alive, through their memories, for another hundred years.

That's why I didn't want to give up so quickly on Ness: Without him, my grandfather's life story would be a little less memorable. I had one more avenue to explore. It entailed talking to Rick Porrello, whose grandfather had been one of the Porrellos shot to death in the cigar store. Rick was a cop in a Cleveland suburb. But at night he wrote expertly researched books about organized crime and ran a Web site about the American mafia. If anyone could tell me about the role the Kravitzes played in Cleveland's corn sugar trade, it would be Rick.

We arranged to meet at the Mad Greek Restaurant, where I had once worked as a bartender. When Rick walked in, I had no trouble recognizing him: With his shaved head, L.A. tan, and faux-alligator loafers, Rick could have been cast in a Hollywood movie as either a wiseguy or a screenwriter.

I was at the bar, on my second tough-guy vodka, when he sat next to me. "Can I buy you a drink?" I asked after introducing myself.

"Thanks," he said. He ordered a cranberry juice on the rocks and explained, "I stopped drinking years ago."

The contradictions in the life of this born-again grandson of gangsters fascinated me. He looked like a wiseguy but drank cranberry juice. He worked as a cop but wrote about the mob. What was his motive in becoming a cop—to redeem his family's blood-soaked past?

"Nah," he told me. "I thought it would be fun."

Clearly, this scion of the notorious Porrellos was not interested in discussing his motivations with me. And, anyway, what I really wanted to know was whether he had ever come across the Kravitz family while researching the book he had written about Cleveland's corn sugar wars.

"Nope, never did," he said. "But that doesn't mean anything. There were lots of Jews in the corn sugar end of the business."

Did any of them get big enough to rival the Lonardos or Porrellos?

"They never lived long enough," he said.

I told Rick about my father—how the Lonardos allegedly kidnapped him, then let him go.

"Didn't happen," Rick said. "Your father would've ended up in a shallow grave. And you wouldn't be here talking with me."

Rick left me with a powerful image: my dad as an infant in a shallow grave. But I wasn't going to share that image with my dad. Too much of my father's sense of himself rested on his "memory" of being kidnapped by the Lonardos. I wanted to use my research as a means of bringing my family closer together. To do that, I needed to keep the focus on the one story that mattered.

"GUESS WHAT?" I wrote Pudge, Harley, and my father. "Nana's story isn't true. On the nights the Porrellos were killed, Ness was in Chicago. And Rick Porrello says he never came across any Kravitzes when he researched his book. I'm beginning to think that Ben and Oscar sold jack to the bootleggers."

My e-mail provoked a swift response, particularly from my father. Within a day I received copies of the following documents from him: Chatza's immigration papers, Ben and Shirley's marriage certificate, a copy of the deed for my grandparent's first home, and Harry's own birth certificate. With them, he made a compelling case of his own: If you took the Porrellos out of my grandmother's story and figured that she had mistakenly linked one event (the Porrellos' murder) with another (Ness's visit), it was possible that Ness barged into Chatza's store some time between April 16, 1934, and November 23, 1936, to set Ben straight.

Harley agreed with that possibility: "Not once did I hear Oscar mention the Porrellos when he told the Ness story." It was clear that none of the Kravitz men were willing to let Ness go. The ice was in the process of being broken.

* * *

NOT EVERYONE AGREED with my inquiry into Ness. When I told a friend of mine in Seattle what I was doing, he got upset: "That's one of my favorite stories of yours," he said. "Why would you even *think* of screwing with it?"

It was a good question. My goal in fact-checking the Ness story was to bring Pudge and Harry closer together. But what if my strategy ended up ruining the Ness story—and robbing it of its power to convey the moral choice my grandpa Benny once made to give up his life of crime? Already, there were no more Porrellos in the story thanks to my fact-checking. What if the story lost Ness? There would be no story at all—and I would end up diminishing my grandfather's stature as the man Ness had marked not as a criminal but as a productive, law-abiding citizen.

It was too late. I had already challenged key elements of the story and taken out the blood and gore of the Porrello murders. On the plus side, Ness was still knocking on Chatza's door—thanks to my dad— which enabled me to pursue the angle that Harley had added to the mix: Did my grandfather give Ness a job after he self-destructed?

From my research, I knew that Ness was as tough on the bad guys in Cleveland as he'd been in Chicago: He raided nightclubs, smashed distilleries, courted the press, and impressed the hell out of Cleveland's reform-minded mayor, who made him the city's director of public safety, or crime czar. In his seven years there, Ness cleaned up Cleveland's notoriously corrupt police department and waged a largely successful war against the gangsters who ran the city's bootlegging, prostitution, and gambling industries.

The one criminal he couldn't take down was the Mad Butcher of Kingsbury Run, a brutal serial killer who terrorized the city by cutting off his victims' heads. The fact that Ness never caught the so-called Torso Murderer tarnished his image. So did his reputation as a playboy, his messy divorce, and a March 5, 1942, car accident that an intoxicated Ness failed to report. Two months later, he was forced to resign.

By then, my thirty-two-year-old grandfather was well on his way to becoming a millionaire. Anchor Rubber, the company he founded, was supplying the U.S. Army with the motor mounts it used in its jeeps, and government contracts were making the Kravitzes rich.

I got a chuckle out of the fact that Ness also worked in the rubber business during the war. He headed the Federal Social Protection Agency in Washington, D.C. His job was to promote abstinence and safe sex and educate military recruits about the dangers of what he called "military saboteur number one." "In war industries," Ness liked to note, "more than 1,200,000 men and women are regularly having to take time off from their work to be treated for syphilis." Ironically, that same disease was killing Ness's old nemesis, Chicago mobster Al Capone.

As the war drew to a close, Ness took a job with an import-export company and became chairman of Diebold Safe and Lock Company in Canton, Ohio. But business bored him. In 1947, he ran as the Republican candidate for mayor of Cleveland—"Vote Yes for Ness" was his slogan—but lost in a landslide. At a time when my grandfather was turning his attention to philanthropy—and to building a rubber-and-tire company in Israel—Ness was nearing the low point of his life.

At this point in my research, I was convinced that there was absolutely no way Ness could have worked for my grandfather in the early 1950s: They were on wildly different paths. But then I read the following passage in Paul Heimel's excellent biography of Ness: "Desperate for employment, Ness called on several old friends in Cleveland, expressing a willingness to accept even a low-paying, menial job to support his wife and son."

According to Heimel, Ness took a job selling electronics for a while. When that ended, he clerked in a downtown bookstore and sold frozen hamburger patties to restaurants. If Ness had set Ben straight, wouldn't my bighearted grandfather have been one of the first people he would have called when he was desperate for a job?

If he had sold electronics and hamburger patties on commission, why couldn't he have done the same thing for motor mounts? I had uncovered a major clue in the mystery of Ness and my grandpa Benny. I felt like Hercule Poirot, Sherlock Holmes, and Miss Marple rolled into one.

But when I e-mailed a description of my breakthrough to Harley, Pudge, and Harry, I didn't get the response I had anticipated.

"There is no way that Eliot Ness worked for Anchor," my dad wrote back. "As Anchor's ASSISTANT COMPTROLLER, then COMPTROLLER, then SECRETARY-TREASURER, I never saw any 'evidence of any transactions' in which Eliot Ness was a company sales Representative. And I do not recall ever seeing Eliot Ness on the Company's PREMISES".

As much as he wanted to preserve the Ness story, my father would never accept an argument based on what he considered faulty information.

"Is it possible that Ness was paid off the books by someone else at the company?" I e-mailed back. Both Harley and Pudge had raised that possibility.

"Prior to my 'appearance on the scene,' such a thing could have happened," my father wrote. "But with the 'internal Accounting Checks and balances' that I 'designed for the Company' with the assistance of my 'ACCOUNTING MENTOR' (Henry Rosewater, CPA), it would have been 'virtually impossible' for Merchandise to leave the Warehouse without being accounted for, Lee!"

AFTER A MONTH of fact-checking, I didn't have a single fact that I could take to the bank. I would have given up on Ness had it not been for the input I kept getting from Harley, Pudge, and Harry, who were more engaged than ever in the story. One day Harley sent me a short autobiography that Ben's youngest brother had written several years before he died. In the manuscript, Tommy recalled the time Ben first instructed him to pick up a load of sugar and sell it on Woodland Avenue all by himself. "It was a hot day and I was sweating like crazy but I took in $18,000," he wrote. "Another time I was making a corn sugar delivery with Eddie, our colored driver, in the Murray Hill section of town. I took the corn sugar around back to the garage. Suddenly gunshots rang out from the barber shop in front." But there was one detail that really caught my attention in the story. Tommy claimed that Chatza bought four new Studebakers with the profits. If Chatza could afford that many brand-new cars, maybe the Kravitzes were much bigger "sugar peddlers" than I had thought.

I e-mailed my theory to Pudge and Harry. Pudge wrote back first. "I have never read Tom's book so I have no idea of the authenticity of his facts. Personally, I have little faith in Tom's truthfulness. I don't believe that Chatza or Dad would have allowed Tom & Ed to make that drop. As for the Studebaker, never heard that one. Knowing Chatza, he wasn't a big spender."

I forwarded Pudge's e-mail to my father, who wrote, "Wow! This is the 'first (1st) time' that I have ever heard (Pun) my Brother make a 'statement like this about his Uncle Tom', Lee! I never knew that he felt the same way as I do about our Uncle."

My father also agreed with what Pudge said about the drop. As for the Studebakers, "Once again I have to 'agree with my Brother.'" he wrote. "I am certain that Chatza NEVER BOUGHT ANYONE A 'NEW CAR' because he, himself, NEVER 'BOUGHT NEW CARS.'"

It was a miracle: Both Pudge and Harry had acknowledged their common perspective on the past. Sure, they hadn't said, "I'm sorry, Pudge," or "I love you, Harry," or made plans to visit each other; nor had they sent e-mails directly to each other, which would probably have been too big and intimidating a step. But they had each uttered the other's name and recognized their brother as a kindred spirit. Without the Ness story and my efforts to fact-check it, there would have been no fraternal "wow."

And then something even more miraculous happened. A few months later, my mother received the first phone call she had gotten in years from Pudge. It came out of nowhere, which led me to believe that the Ness story had helped prompt it. Pudge and my mother talked for more than an hour. They updated each other on their health and kids, and Pudge said that he would be moving from California to Denver soon to be closer to his grandchildren.

Pudge's main reason for calling was to tell my mother that he had always liked her and that he didn't hate my father. "He said he never felt like he had a brother," my mother told me. "And he thought that Harry got all the attention, which I already knew."

"So what did you say?"

"I told him that what matters is that brothers have a past together, that they have blood together, that they should see each other before they die," my mother said.

"And how did Pudge respond?" I asked.

"He said that he was thinking of writing your dad."

And then a month or so later, Pudge called my mother again. This time he wanted her to know that he doesn't like to write long e-mails like he imagined Harry does. I am sure he knew that my mother would convey this message to my father, and that my father would be at least a little more likely to curb his sermonizing as a result.

So Pudge e-mailed my father a short, friendly birthday greeting. How do I know? Because my dad copied me on his e-mail back to Pudge: "Thank you for 'remembering me' on my Birthday, this year, Pudge! Phyllis mentioned to me that you 'don't like long E-mail Messages' so I will try to 'keep this one' as 'short as possible.' Because I do not use a 'Telephone,' my E-mail Messages are 'composed like a Telephone conversation.'"

Since college, I had received over a thousand letters from my father, typically one a week. My father's letters were so idiosyncratic in their use of quotation marks, parentheses, and exclamation points that I used to show them to my roommates and girlfriends, who would try to penetrate what they called "his secret code." For nearly forty years, I had been befuddled my father's letters, as had everyone else who received them. But now the method behind his madness was clear. He constructed his letters to replicate the dynamic he might have on a telephone if he were able to hear. His idiosyncratic formatting wasn't as cold and bureaucratic as it seemed; it was meant to encourage intimacy.

What follows is the most intimate conversation that two brothers had had in more than thirty years:

Well, Harry, you hit the big 77 yesterday.

Hard to "comprehend", but I am "<u>enthralled</u>" with having received the "<u>opportunity</u>" to have "<u>made it to this point</u>", Pudge!

Florida must be keeping you young.

"Where we live" in Florida and the "lifestyle" of the "Villagers" definitely is a "contributing factor" to being able to "extend one's life". It is a "People Community" made up of Residents from "every walk of life". When one meets someone, the only "questions that are asked" are:

(1) Where did you "come from"?

(2) Do you play "Golf"?

Spoke to Phyllis today and she tells me that at 77 you're doing OK.

Compared to "most 77+ year olds", I cannot really "complain", Pudge! I contribute my "longevity in life" to:

(1) "Marching to my own Drum" and not trying to be "someone that I really would not be happy being".

(2) Being "very disciplined" with respect to avoiding things that would be "detrimental to my physical well being" (e.g., Smoking, drinking, eating habits, exercise regimen, etc.).

(3) Maintaining "control over my emotions" (even under the "most trying conditions").

(4) Working "very long and hard" to achieve "personal goals" that I had "established" with respect to providing for Phyllis and my Sons.

Please understand that I was never angry with you.

I never "thought" that you were "angry" at me, Pudge. No matter what "others told me", I felt that we both were "victims of a Childhood that we had to "share" with so many other Family Members beyond the "immediate Family".

Let's be glad that we have both made it this far.

Believe me when I say to you that I am "very glad" that we have BOTH "made it so far" considering the "many physical problems" that we have had to "overcome" during our respective lives".

Since I have never been one to "live in the past", I "sincerely hope" that this "resumption of communication" will be a "new beginning" for both of us". I will always be your "older Brother" in both "heart and mind". . . . . . . Harry.

When I read this exchange, I felt like crying. In this single correspondence, my father and his brother had traveled 90 percent of the distance they needed to on their journey toward reconciliation. Ness had broken the ice and enabled me to push and prod them. But now it was up to the two brothers to complete their journey. They had two thousand miles to go, the distance from Denver, Colorado, to Ocala, Florida. One of them would need to get on an airplane; the other would need to meet him at the airport. It was not a reconciliation that could occur in an hour or a day; it would take two or three days of memories, meals, and laughter to even begin to reestablish trust. I could just imagine how light they would feel as the weight of all those years of avoiding each other fell from their shoulders.

Would this final reconciliation ever happen? I couldn't be sure. But for now, I could rejoice in the fact that the brothers had e-mailed each other directly and that my father had become less of a mystery to me and my mother: "All these years I've been thinking that your father was queer by writing back to people in red," she wrote me. "Now it makes a lot of sense to me. For Harry, it's like he's talking on the telephone."

CHAPTER NINE

I Remember Nana

Eulogizing a Loved One

WHEN MY GRANDMOTHER died, I didn't attend her funeral. We were still mourning Elizabeth's brother, who had been killed in a car accident, and couldn't imagine dealing with more sadness.

My aunt Fern had been institutionalized and nobody seemed to know or care where she was. Pudge and my father weren't talking. My grandmother had spent the last six months in a hospice, wasting away from Alzheimer's disease. I didn't want to remember her that way or get distracted by my family's problems. So I stayed away.

But there was something I missed out on by not attending my grandmother's funeral. I never said good-bye to her.

And now, as my year of completing my unfinished business was coming to an end, I felt myself being drawn, as if by a powerful magnet, back to Nana Shirley. I wanted to tell her what she meant to me with a loving, grateful heart.

IT WAS MIDMORNING when I parked my rental car at the cemetery and walked through the front gate. My memory told me to go a quarter mile down the main path, but instead I took an immediate right. I let myself be led by the magnetic force. Within seconds, I was standing in front of her grave.

The row of Kravitzes faced a busy intersection near I-271, the highway that ran through Cleveland's eastern suburbs. Across the street I could see a BP station at which the price of gas had risen to a shocking $3.11 per gallon, and also a Chrysler dealership that was liquidating its inventory. It was ironic that the Kravitzes had a front-row seat at the demise of the industry that had once made them rich.

I turned around and looked down at five slabs of polished granite:

OSCAR KRAVITZ (1912–1987)

ROSE KRAVITZ (1916–1981)

BESSIE PLATT (1881–1966)

SHIRLEY KRAVITZ (1910–1995)

BEN KRAVITZ (1909–1972)

So much love and heartache, all in a row: the brothers who built a rubber-and-tire empire, then watched it fall apart; the sisters who married the brothers and spent their last decades not talking to each other; the mother who put three of her five children, including Rose, in an orphanage after her husband died.

Walking from grave to grave, I felt saddened by it all—by all the love and possibility that once existed between these people, by the fact that, in death, they stared at a sign that said: LIQUIDATION SALE! EVERYTHING MUST GO! After so much pain and sorrow—after the years in the orphanage and the demise of the tire company and the grudge that persisted between Shirley and Rose until the day they died—why would they choose to spend eternity in such close proximity to each other? It was a silly question: They were family.

My grandparents were surrounded by their closest relatives, but they were also buried in the same neighborhood as their friends: the Sherwins and Ratners, the Garbers and Cohens, the Kleinmans and Adelmans, the people who had worked, vacationed, and prayed with them, who had shared their sorrows and their joy.

If you taped a photo of each of these people to the top of their grave and looked down from one hundred feet in the air, you would get a fairly accurate picture of my grandmother's Facebook page had she had one. It gave me great comfort to imagine her kibitzing, even in death, with her yenta friends.

In ways I was envious of Shirley and her friends for having lived in the same community their entire lives. Day after day, they were part of each other's ongoing life narrative. They were perhaps the last generation that could say, "We had old-world relationships. Our deepest human connections lasted from the cradle to the grave."

I HAD BEEN afraid that my grandmother's epic disputes would detour me from starting my own family with Elizabeth. That was perhaps my main reason for not attending her funeral. But twelve years later, after I lost my job, it was clear that my success in becoming a better husband, father, and son was linked, in part, to completing the unfinished emotional business that stemmed from those Kravitz family dramas. And so, I started searching for Sorrow's daughter, my aunt Fern. And I used the story my grandmother had told me about Eliot Ness to break the ice between my father and Uncle Pudge.

Because my grandmother was such a significant part of these journeys, I got to know and understand her better. Nana Shirley was born into difficult circumstances: After her father died, her mother had a nervous breakdown and Shirley had to quit school to work in a bakery to support her family. At twelve, she was working fifteen hours a day so that she could get her siblings out of the orphanage. If she had been educated and lived today, my grandmother could have been CEO of a major corporation. That's how competent, charismatic, and persuasive she could be. But her constant, gnawing narcissism—her need to always get the credit and be the heroine of everyone's story—left her children and many of the people in her circle feeling abandoned and alone.

Like most people with strong public personas, my grandmother provoked strong feelings; there were people who loved her and people who hated her.

I loved her.

I loved my grandmother for taking on the burden of Fern when the doctors urged her to lock Fern away. I loved her stories, how she embellished them with Yiddishisms and would end them by invoking Judaism's just, omniscient God.

I loved my grandmother for making my *meshuga* father *plotz*, for *kvelling* about me when I graduated college, for teaching me to protect my *shmattes* with mothballs. I loved the way she talked about "my darling, my Benny," as she called him. No one could tell my grandfather's story as well as she could—how he built the business and raised millions of dollars for Israel by speaking from his heart. She wasn't interested in any other man. "I had a *beau-ti-ful* life with my Benny," she said. "I really did. I met him when I was a young girl. God was good. And sent him to me."

My grandmother could be stubborn and vindictive. As a result, she had a long list of unfinished business when she died, including two items at the top of my own list. After I had completed those items, I could stand at her grave and report some family news she would have loved to hear:

"Fern is getting excellent care, and she is playing the piano again. Pudge and Harry are in good health and keeping in good touch. You'll be happy to know that Elizabeth and I named our first son 'Benjamin,' after Grandpa Benny, and that our three children say the Sabbath prayers on Friday night over the candles, challah, and wine. Our store-bought rotisserie chicken tastes nothing like the ones you made and we only have homemade matzo ball soup on Passover, but we are doing the best we can, given our complicated lives, to carry on the traditions that mattered so much to you and Grandpa."

It felt good to report these things to my grandmother, but it would have felt a lot better had she been alive. Because we want so badly for our loved ones to live forever, we assume we'll see them tonight, tomorrow, or the next day—and then the next day doesn't come. Something terrible happens. My high school girlfriend and Elizabeth's brother were both killed in car accidents. Andre's daughter was murdered by insurgents in Iraq. I have had friends die of cancer and other diseases long before they should have.

Mark 13:33 warns: "Take heed, watch, for you know not when the time will come."

If we remembered how we could be separated from our loved ones at any moment, we would accumulate a lot less unfinished business. We would be quicker to forgive each other, and be more kind. We would eulogize each other now, instead of waiting for death.

As I stood at my grandmother's grave, I began thinking about my mother and father in their late seventies. Of the people I loved, they were the closest, statistically, to the end of their lives. Did they have any idea what they meant to me, or what I'd miss most about them when they were gone?

When I was three, my father made me practice my pitcher's windup fifteen minutes a day in front of a mirror. When I was five, he threw a ball up in the air until it hit me in the head, and as I stood there crying, he told me, "Now you know that there's nothing to be afraid of." When I was in high school, he told me to "push through the pain and keep playing," even when my nose was broken or my pitching arm ached. I wanted to make him proud, but hated him for bringing so much pain into my life. And I resented my mother for trying to protect me from the pain, for worrying so much, because I thought that her worrying jinxed me and would make me less strong.

I was convinced, as I grew older, that my parents didn't understand my need to travel, write, and find my way in the world. I felt like I was a terrible disappointment to them—the son who should have been a doctor.

I was wrong, of course. I could have become a doctor, lawyer, or president of a bank and they would have loved me the same, which was a lot, and been there whenever I needed them. If they died tomorrow, would they know the ways they had enriched my life? Standing at my grandmother's grave, I realized that the journeys of the past year had strengthened my desire to give my parents the credit I had too often withheld.

I would want my father to know that as much as I resisted the intensity of his coaching I finally saw it for what it was: an expression of his love. I would want my mother to know how glad I was to have a mother that cared.

I would want both of them to know that one of my prized possessions was a snapshot of them frolicking on the beach. They were maybe nineteen at the time, and about to be married. With her perfect smile, my mother was movie-star beautiful. And from the way he held her, it was clear how smitten my father was. Young, beautiful, in love—these were my parents in the months before they conceived me. Some people spend their whole lives looking for evidence that their parents loved them. I could see it in this photograph, and in the way they loved my children. Watching my father play hide-and-seek with the twins, listening to my mother talk about Noah's smile, I reveled in their joy. What would I miss most about my parents? Experiencing my children through their eyes.

CHAPTER TEN

The Circle Grows Wider

Keeping a Promise

HAVE YOU EVER made a promise and failed to keep it? I've probably made and broken hundreds of them over the years. But the one
that gnawed at me the most as I attended to my unfinished business
was a promise I made to a boy in a Kenyan refugee camp in 1994.

It was a volatile time in sub-Saharan Africa. A third of its forty-
eight countries were embroiled in wars and recently the presidents
of Rwanda and Burundi had both been killed in a plane crash. That
month the UN World Food Program had fed 270,000 refugees and
550,000 drought victims in the region.

Before I left on my trip, I had been inoculated against diphthe-
ria, typhoid, yellow fever, tetanus, and polio and packed a ten-day
supply of malaria pills. On the flight from London to Nairobi, I
read a guidebook on Kenya and taught myself some very basic Swahili: *Asante* (Thank you); *Sangapi?* (What time is it?); *Hakuna matata*
(No problem).

I had traveled to Kenya to attend an international social studies
conference. At the time I edited several current events magazines used
in classrooms. The conference would give me an opportunity to learn
about the challenges Africans faced in making the transition from
postcolonialist dictatorships to multiparty democracies. We would be
hearing from political leaders and scholars, but I also wanted to see
Africa's struggles with my own eyes. I arranged to spend a morning at
the National Assembly watching Kenya's parliament in session, and
then an afternoon shadowing a program that worked with Nairobi's
street children. I also hoped to visit a refugee camp.

The head of the United Nations High Commissioner for Refugees media office in Nairobi said I was in luck: The morning after the conference ended, there would be a UNHCR supply plane headed up to Kakuma, a refugee camp in the northwestern region of Kenya, near the borders of Uganda and southeastern Sudan. I could hitch a ride up and back that same day, giving me enough time to tour the camp and talk with aid workers and refugees.

The plane's pilot had been a captain in Britain's Royal Air Force. He invited me to sit next to him in the cockpit. As we headed north, he pointed out Mt. Kenya rising seventeen thousand feet high in the east, and the Great Rift Valley, with its patchwork of arid desert and fertile farmland. When Lake Turkana came into view, the pilot swooped down to one hundred or so feet to see the pink flamingos wading in its shallows. The sound of our propellers spooked the birds and waves upon waves of them rose up, jostling the plane. The pilot struggled to regain control. Later he admitted how close we had come to crashing.

We landed at a small airstrip near the town of Kakuma—Swahili for "nowhere." The average daily temperature was 104 degrees Fahrenheit, and the area was prone to blinding dust storms. We headed by jeep to the camp. The driver pointed out where a dust storm had recently closed the road, cutting off supplies to the camp. "Watch out for spiders, scorpions, and snakes—they are poisonous," he said. A sprawling expanse of huts came into view. We had arrived at the refugee camp. Like a prison camp, it was separated from the desert by concertina wire.

The camp had been started eighteen months earlier and housed nearly thirty-seven thousand refugees. Most of them were children and teenagers. We cleared security. Aid workers were distributing bags of beans, rice, and sorghum to a long line of refugee women. Relief workers from organizations like CARE, the International Rescue Committee, and UNICEF moved about the camp. From their accents, I could tell that these idealistic young people came from a variety of countries: Canada, the United States, France, Australia, and Greece. Even in this scorching heat, they exuded energy and good humor. I had been to other refugee camps and knew how the mood of the aid workers could darken. Buy them a beer and they would complain about the shortages of food and medical supplies at Kakuma. They would question the value of the work they were doing. They would plead for the world to care more about these children.

Along the broad dirt road that cut through the center of the camp, there was a makeshift marketplace of wooden shacks: Some of the shacks sold coffee, tea, and stationery; most just offered shade and a place to listen to the radio and sit. Colorful, hand-drawn signs advertised LA LIBERIA RESTAURANT, THE TWINS HOTEL, the TAPE AND RADIO REPAIR shop. In the brutally hot air, a group of teenage boys kicked around a soccer ball; a crowd of younger children cheered them on.

One of the aid workers accompanied me into a neighborhood dense with refugees from Somalia. It was there that I met the boy whose face I would never forget. It wasn't a beautiful face. It had been hardened by the destruction of his village, the loss of his mother, father, and other relatives, and the long journey he had taken by foot and truck to Kakuma. But it lit up whenever he smiled or asked a question.

It was hard to tell how old he was; with a shift in the light, he could seem thirteen, sixteen, or twenty-one years of age. He was wearing a bright yellow T-shirt with the phrase AFRICA '92 on it, referring, I supposed, to some athletic contest. He prodded me to tell him about American football, how it differed from soccer, his favorite sport. We walked to the hut he shared with his three best friends. It had a thatched roof and dirt floor. The boy brought out a piece of cardboard for me to sit on. As he brewed a pot of tea for us, I looked around. The walls were papered with articles and ads from British magazines, mainly pretty girls and soccer stars. It created a sad contrast between the dreams of these boys and the reality of their lives.

My host took me to see Kakuma's new library. He went there every day to read and improve his English. I was surprised to see that there was only a handful of books on the shelves. Most of them were textbooks that had been published in the 1940s and 1950s, when the British ruled Kenya. I couldn't imagine how anyone could learn anything current or useful from them.

Again, I was struck by the gulf between the boy's desire to educate himself and the paltry resources available to him. Like millions of young people throughout the world, he sought a better life. I could see him excelling in school and working hard to make a living. Despite the circumstances of his life, he was generous to his neighbors and took pride in his community. Had he lived in an American suburb, he might have become a member of the city council or school board, or run the voting booth on election day. Would he get that chance? Was there anything I could do to help him?

"It's a very nice library," I said. "But I think it could use more books. When I get back to New York, I'll send you books about sports and science and famous people. I'll get the library an encyclopedia and dictionaries and novels and interesting magazines that will help you improve your English."

I expected him to smile and express his gratitude; instead, he shrugged his shoulders and looked embarrassed by my offer.

"That's what everyone says," he reluctantly said.

"I really mean it," I said. "I'll fill this library with books."

LOOKING BACK, I had every intention of doing what I said I'd do. I worked for a large publishing company. I ran magazines read by millions of students. I had used those resources to put together partnerships that resulted in student town meetings on C-Span, a lyric-writing contest with Jackson Browne, current-events videos with NBC News, a project that would enable America's school-children to chat via computer with explorer Will Steger as he traversed the Arctic in a dogsled.

Buoyed by these successes, I didn't doubt my ability to fill Kakuma's library. I even had a plan. I would ask the company I worked for to donate a thousand books to the library. A charity-minded airline could fly them to Nairobi, where the UNHCR could pick them up and shuttle them to Kakuma. For publicity, I'd want to get a photograph of the director of the camp reading a children's book to a group of young refugees; also one of a teen who dreamed of becoming a doctor holding a biology book. I'd publish an article about the Kakuma "book lift" in my magazines, giving everyone involved a reason to feel proud.

As soon as I returned to New York, I made a few phone calls and realized that orchestrating the book donation would be a lot more complicated than I had anticipated. I'd need to make my case to decision makers at five organizations and navigate several levels of bureaucracy in the United States and Kenya. If I had had a few weeks to focus exclusively on the project, I might have been able to accomplish what needed to be done. I didn't have that much time. Like other visitors who had made promises to the boy in Kakuma, I would end up letting him down.

FOR THE NEXT thirteen years, I didn't think at all about the boy. My job as a magazine editor gave me other opportunities to become involved in worthwhile campaigns, and my promise to him got buried in my pile of other well-meaning projects that hadn't worked out. Then in 2007, on a brisk spring morning in Washington, D.C., the boy pricked at my conscience. I was giving a talk called "Making a Difference through Journalism" to one hundred high school journalists from all over the United States, and a girl from Minnesota asked me if there had been any causes I had wanted to cover in my career, but didn't.

Without losing a beat, I said, "No, but there's a promise I once made to a boy in a refugee camp and I didn't keep it." Because my talk was aired on C-Span, I could see on tape how surprised and even shaken I was by my answer. I hadn't thought about that boy in years. But now I was telling a hundred young Americans and C-Span's cable audience how bad I felt for not having made the difference I should have made in his life. It was as if the boy had come to represent all of the world's marginalized and vulnerable children to me. His message to me was "Don't forget us."

Even when you're not aware of it on a day-to-day basis, your unfinished business weighs down your soul. Then one day, when you least expect it, it makes itself known.

WHEN I COMPILED my list of unfinished business, my promise to the boy was near the top. At first I resolved to fill Kakuma's library with books. But as the year went on, I found myself backing away from the project. It had grown more complicated: I no longer ran a magazine; my contacts at the UNHCR had moved on to other places; it was harder, as a "mere citizen," to get decision makers at publishing companies and airlines to take my calls. And the truth was, I couldn't even be sure that Kakuma's library still needed books.

In retrospect, my promise to the boy had partially been motivated by my desire to do something big and impressive. I had been on a crusade at the time, and I had trouble thinking small. If I had been less driven, I might have made a lesser, more achievable promise. It took me a long time to come to this realization, to understand that scale matters. As my year of doing good was coming to an end, I had done absolutely nothing for the refugee children in Kakuma. But I was thinking smaller, and doing so had begun to energize me. In the coming weeks, I would need to make the transition from my year off to my ongoing life. This idea of scale, of not biting off more than you can chew, of keeping your priorities straight and in balance, would be key.

BECAUSE WE WANT our children to be good and active citizens when they grow up, Elizabeth and I have developed two rituals they've come to enjoy. On election day, they accompany us into the booth and help us select the candidates we'll support; then they pull the lever. Our other citizenship ritual occurs on the day after Thanksgiving. After breakfast, we clear the dining room table and sort through the fifty or so solicitation letters we've received from foundations and charities. Elizabeth hands each of the children an envelope with $100 in it. You can imagine how quickly they open up their wad of twenty-, ten-, and five-dollar bills and revel in their wealth. But then it's time for them to become philanthropists. The kids identify their favored causes and charities and give us their reasons for supporting them.

This year, it was no surprise that all three children said "Alzheimer's" when Elizabeth asked them for their causes. Two months earlier, their grandma Joyce had died after a heartbreaking battle with the disease. Even when she no longer remembered their names, the children had visited her at least twice a week in her home in the hospice. Caroline asked the nurses if we could bring our dog Pip to cheer the patients up. "When Grandma was on the Alzheimer's floor, it looked like everyone there was so sad," she said. Ben had another reason for wanting to donate money to the Alzheimer's Association. "There's not a lot known about the disease," he said. "Whatever research they can do will be important."

Noah and Caroline were moved to help the homeless. There had been more homeless people on the streets and the subway lately, and just the other day Noah had given a bagel from his lunch box to a man begging on our street corner. Caroline had befriended a man in blue overalls who swept the sidewalks near her school. "He used to be homeless," she said. "But now he gets paid $7.40 an hour to keep the streets clean. He's really nice. And he's always saying how he's 'ready, willing, and able.'" That was the motto of the Doe Fund, the group that had given the man the job. "I'm going to give twenty dollars to the Doe Fund," Caroline said.

"Anything else on your minds?" Elizabeth asked.

Ben said cancer research because Coach John, his baseball manager, was undergoing chemotherapy for stage 4 colon cancer. He also suggested helping paralyzed veterans. "There are all these veterans coming back wounded from Iraq and Afghanistan," he explained. "Also, we should do it in honor of Grandpa Ted." Ben was referring to Elizabeth's father, who had lost his arm in the Battle of the Bulge. He died long before the kids were born, but they were all proud of him.

Noah had two special causes: "We should give to the trees, Pops. Without them there wouldn't be furniture, paper, or oxygen. We couldn't live." He also liked the idea of giving to an animal shelter. "Because of Mac," he explained. When we adopted Mac a few months earlier, the puppy was only a few days from being killed. The thought of Mac dead was intolerable for all of us.

As my kids discussed their charities, it struck me how different triggers could move them to care about the same cause. Both Ben and Caroline wanted to support a charity that addressed the needs of "inner-city kids with less opportunity," as Ben said. Ben's trigger had been the trailer he'd seen for the movie *Precious*, about an abused girl who wasn't given the encouragement to read and express herself until she was sixteen. Caroline had her own *Precious*: the sixth-grade boy she was mentoring at her school. "He has to go super slowly," she explained. "So we read out loud to each other. It's fun. And it makes me feel mature." That week the boy had thanked her for the first time. "It was a huge deal for him," she said. "He's really smart and he really wants to do better in school, but his friends want him to act like they do, like he doesn't care."

Listening to my children—hearing Noah talk about Mac and Caroline tell stories about the boy she was mentoring at school and the man who swept the street corner—gave me a new perspective on how I wanted to live my life. Before, I had a tendency to do good by orchestrating grand and complicated projects. Those can be fine, but not if they become so big that they never get done, so consuming that they distract me from my kids, and so "important" that they keep me from seeing the hundreds of smaller opportunities for doing good that present themselves to me each and every day. By opening the door for an elderly lady, by looking a stranger in the eye, by attuning myself to what Wordsworth called those "little, nameless, unremembered acts of kindness and of love," I can become a better person and contribute to making this a better world. I can do more, too. But a lot can be accomplished by doing the right things now in the rhythm of your life.

At the end of our annual giving ritual, I told my children about the promise I had broken to the boy in the refugee camp. They felt bad for that boy—and for all the children who had been orphaned and left homeless from Africa's wars. Ben said he was donating a total of forty dollars to Doctors Without Borders and the Mercy Corps, two organizations he liked that volunteered in Africa's refugee camps. Noah also donated money to help refugees. But it was Caroline who came up with the idea that eased my conscience. She suggested that we go to a bookstore and buy some children's books that Kakuma's library probably didn't have yet. "We'll buy a boxful, then send it," she said. Caroline volunteered to decorate the box and make a card for the librarian. She suggested that we include a picture of the refugee boy. "Maybe he's still there," she said. "Maybe the librarian will know him, or remember his name. I'll ask her to make a card that says, 'These books were donated in the boy's name.'" It was a brilliant idea and one we could accomplish in less than a day.

Moving Ahead
The Journey of a Lifetime

THE CANADA GEESE have returned to the lake. During the warm days and freezing nights, they troll for small fish and seaweed and fill the air with gruff honking noises. Soon they'll fly off in an elegant V formation, their sights set south.

A year ago I wanted to fly off with them, away from a job and life that no longer made sense to me. I no longer feel this way. I sit by the fireplace and pour myself a glass of port wine. It is ruby red, fermented with grapes leaves, cherries, and plums. I snack from a plate of Brie, Klamath River smoked salmon, and chocolate macadamia nuts. The wine and salmon were gifts from Bishop Auxentios and the monks; the macadamias came from Andre and his wife, Vicki. That I'm sitting before this fire, enjoying these gifts from my friends, suggests a change in me. A year ago, I would have been too distracted to savor this moment. Consumed by work and then by not working, I would have found it impossible for me to count or take pleasure in my blessings.

In the warmth of this fire, I feel grateful: for this day, for my family, for the choice I made a year ago to complete the unfinished business of my life.

WHEN I STARTED out, I had no idea what lay ahead. The situations that become our unfinished business are messy and complicated. They also involve our deepest fears. I had always been afraid of failing and letting people down, of doing the wrong thing and embarrassing myself. I was also afraid of being a bad father and an ungrateful son. Those fears weighed me down and held me back, both at work and in my relationships. They contributed to my becoming someone who worked compulsively, putting my job ahead of everything else.

When I started out, I defined my unfinished business in terms of closing circles and making amends. It was a matter of doing things I should have done and reconnecting with old friends. Father Jarvis helped me to see it in larger terms: "We are all on Death Row and we are all dying," he said. "And that reality should awaken in each of us a sense of urgency." When you realize that you can die at any moment, you feel compelled to do the important things in your life now and keep your unfinished business to a minimum.

Akmal, my psychologist friend, gave me another way of looking at it: "Our unfinished business isn't about resting in peace," he said. "It's about moving forward. It's about optimizing our potential as human beings." According to Akmal, we have a fixed amount of energy available to us each day for getting things done. By not resolving our unfinished business, we deplete that energy. You start the day with ten kilograms of psychological energy. But the kids are being annoying at breakfast, so you leave the house without kissing them good-bye. Suddenly you're down to nine kilograms of energy for the day. Your wife reminds you to make an appointment for your annual physical. You know what the doctor is going to say— lose fifteen pounds, the same thing he said a year ago. So you put off making the appointment, risking an argument with your wife. Subtract two more kilograms of energy. And so on . . . until you're down to five kilograms of energy for the day and you have to work twice as hard to get the same tasks done.

Allowing your unfinished business to accumulate is a bad thing. It makes you tired and irritable. Lessening your load causes the opposite to happen. When I found my aunt, saw Andre, mailed that check to John, and eulogized my grandmother, I experienced a surge of energy. I became more focused and got more done. I was a more giving person. I had more fun.

And I felt more whole: Fern awakened my empathetic side, John stirred up my thirst for adventure, Auxentios engaged my capacity to look inward. I could see the various parts of me for what they were. They didn't fight as much for my attention. They were more in tune. When I started out, I had no idea that I'd end up feeling so much more complete and whole.

I TOOK TEN separate journeys to complete the ten items on my list. Yet on each journey, I found myself taking side trips and detours that yielded their own unexpected rewards.

When I was trying to unravel the mystery of Ness and my grandfather, I spent an afternoon photographing the abandoned block-long building that had once housed Anchor Rubber, my grandfather's company. It was sobering to see the shattered windows and scurrying rats, but as I looked through the lens of my camera, I imagined my grandfather walking from one end of the plant to the other, savoring the smell of newly manufactured floor mats. It's an image I'll treasure.

I was in a stationery store, looking for a gift for Fern. When I turned around, I saw my secret crush from grade school, standing behind the cash register. I thought about approaching her, then lost my nerve. On my next trip to the store, I presented Laurel with a copy of the poem I had written for her when I was twelve years old. Over forty years later, it made her day.

On that same trip I visited Joyce's mother. I had kept my distance from Anita because I didn't want to make her sad. But she was delighted to see me and we ended up reminiscing about Joyce for more than two hours. We remembered how much she had loved photographing circuses and kids, how she got excited by new challenges, how she became one of the first camerawomen in network news. Anita, who was nearing ninety, seemed to grow younger and younger as we talked about her daughter. I did too. Hugging Anita good-bye, perhaps for the last time, I felt as happy as I had been when I first hugged Fern. Sometimes you don't realize how much you needed to get closure until it happens.

ALBERT EINSTEIN ONCE said that "A human being is part of a whole, called by us 'Universe,' a part limited by time and space." Yet we experience our thoughts and feelings as "something separate from the rest." Einstein viewed this self-centric way of looking at the world as "a kind of optical delusion."

Time and again, I became aware of how my "optical delusions" created unfinished business for me. I was convinced that Anita would get sad, that John was still mad, and that Andre wouldn't remember me, so I put off seeing them. But when I reached out to them it turned out that the opposite was true: Anita was delighted to see me again, John had absolutely no memory of the six hundred dollars I owed him, Andre remembered me and my fastball too. I had avoided approaching these people because I could only see their thoughts and feelings through a single lens—my own. Einstein considered our optical delusions "a kind of prison . . . Our task must be to free ourselves from this prison by widening our circle of compassion to embrace all living creatures and the whole of nature in its beauty." When we keep our promises, when we bury our grudges, when we make a point of being thoughtful and kind, when we really listen to what other people are saying, our circle widens to embrace more people. I might not have embraced the whole of nature, but I found myself in a much richer place—that of true human connectedness.

FOR THE PAST year I been able to live and think according to my own timetable. I haven't had to work in an office or manage a staff.

I have gone wherever my unfinished business has taken me. When I have needed to write, Elizabeth has encouraged me to stay alone in the country, where I can wrestle with my thoughts for days at a time and celebrate each new breakthrough by relaxing in front of a warm crackling fire.

My extraordinary year is over; I am about to return to my ordinary life and its pressures. Faced with the challenges of looking for a job and making a living, how can I keep my load lean and my unfinished business from accumulating? I want to maintain the rich relationships I have rekindled with Fern, Andre, and my father, and deepen other friendships and bonds. But how will I be able to do this in a world that offers a husband, father, and citizen so little time?

I'll need to make the time. When it comes to the small stuff, like fixing the mailbox or calling my parents, I'll "just do it," as Elizabeth says. I won't let the little tasks grow into huge, impossible burdens. As for the bigger projects, I'll need to keep reminding myself to scale down my promises and good intentions to what I can reasonably achieve. Once a workaholic, always a workaholic. But I pledge to slow down and turn off the treadmill before I start getting overwhelmed, and to schedule regular periods of silence and reflection so that I can quiet my fears and count my blessings.

YESTERDAY WAS ONE of those blessings. Caroline asked me to help her with the first research paper she had ever written. It was for her seventh-grade humanities class. Her topic was "John Smith and His Leadership of Jamestown." She was given chapters from three college textbooks to use. Understandably, she struggled with the material. Before she could write the paper, she needed to understand the ingredients that made communities successful, including strong and consistent leadership, shared goals, and assigning the right people to the right tasks. The Jamestown colony had been failing before Smith became its leader, and once he left it, it started to fail again.

Why had Smith been able to turn it around? Were there other factors that contributed to his success? These were difficult concepts for Caroline and I'm sure most kids her age to grasp, and my first instinct was to rush in and rescue my daughter from her distress. But then I remembered what Father Jarvis said: Love takes work. It can be inconvenient and time-consuming. It requires that you put yourself in the other person's shoes before acting.

I spent the next three hours serving as a sounding board for my daughter. It took her that long to wrestle with the material and write a paper that reflected what she had learned and digested. She kept telling me, "Don't give me words, Dad, just give me feedback." She wanted the work to be entirely her own. And it was. I was proud of her. And I think that she appreciated the time and support I gave her. We achieved a new level of trust.

Afterward, I went to the cafe down the street for lunch. Don, the proprietor of the cafe, only uses ingredients that are produced by local farmers. The hot dog, brioche bun, salad, and sauerkraut I ate were all raised, grown, or milled within a mile of where we live. Don has much bigger plans for the cafe, and he showed me the brochure he had designed to promote his ideas for helping the local economy. It was way too wordy, so I offered to edit it for him. A year ago, I wouldn't have done that. And if I had, the project would have started so low on my to-do list that I would have never have gotten around to doing it. But now—and in my life going forward—I plan on assigning a much higher priority to opportunities like these and other "little nameless unremembered acts of kindness." Helping a child with her homework or a neighbor to achieve his dreams are acts that deeply matter.

There was a wonderful I-Thou quality to my encounters with Caroline and Don yesterday. I didn't see them as simply Caroline my daughter and Don the farmer, or as Caroline the student and Don the cafe owner. I experienced them as individuals with fears and ambitions, seriousness and good humor, behaviors and idiosyncrasies that made them interesting, endearing, and unique. I was aware of the sound of their voices and the way the changing light of day played on their features. I was alert to them, and they seemed alert to me.

Something else was going on. It had to do with the way I was seeing myself. Usually I see myself in a singular role—for example, husband, father, editor, son. But yesterday I was thinking of myself as a Thou, as someone who could relate in his truest, fullest humanity to another human being. When you experience yourself that way, it's hard to imagine yourself becoming a workaholic again, defined solely by your job. Think of yourself as a Thou and not an It and you will make the time and expend the energy to do the right things on an ongoing basis, keeping your unfinished business to a minimum.

All of us have unfinished business. It can be a friend we lost touch with or a mentor we never thanked; it can be a call we meant to make or a pledge we failed to honor. It can be a goal we lost sight of or a spiritual quest we put on hold. Too often, life takes over and pushes the experiences that might enrich, enlarge, or even complete us to the bottom of our to-do list.

The hurdles we face in tackling our unfinished business can seem impossibly high, but the first step in clearing them is usually quite simple: Write an e-mail or make a phone call. You can never tell when the weight you've been shouldering will slip away, leaving you a more complete and loving person.

Questions for Discussion

These discussion questions are designed to enhance your group's conversation about *Unfinished Business*, the inspiring story of one man's extraordinary year of trying to do the right things.

1. Why does the author embark on his year-long project? What does he hope to accomplish by tying up his life's loose ends?

2. The author lists several reasons why he lets important matters slide: not enough time or energy, his tendency to procrastinate, his fear of doing the wrong thing. What are some of the reasons that *you* accumulate unfinished business?

3. The author writes that his family is the source of his "most intimate and anxiety-producing" unfinished business (14). Do you think that's true for most people? Is it true for you?

4. The author goes on ten journeys to close circles or make amends. Which of his journeys—for example, paying back a debt, finding a long-lost relative, thanking an old teacher—resonated most with you? Why?

5. If you had one year to tie up your loose emotional ends, how would you spend it? What items would be at the top of *your* list of unfinished business?

6. Shahid believes that it's important to address your unfinished business because "we need to make an accounting of these things before we die, so that our souls can rest"; Akmal says, "It's not about resting in peace. It's about moving forward. It's about optimizing your human potential" (92). Who in your opinion is right?

7. Think of all the people you cared about who have passed away. Did any of them die without knowing what they meant to you? If you were able to have one more conversation with those people, what would you say to them?

8. The author says that he wants to live "a more connected life" (125). What does he mean by that phrase? Rate your own life: On a scale of 1 to 10, how rich is it in terms of human connectedness?

9. Mr. Jarvis challenges his students by saying: "After you die, what would you like people to say about you? Your answer to that question should guide the way you live" (137). What would you like people to say about *you* after you die?

10. Has this book given you a perspective on your own life that you find useful? What ideas are you likely to take away or apply from it? Can you think of any steps you can take to keep yourself from accumulating unfinished business?

Readers Share Their Own "Unfinished Business" Stories

In the months since this book has been published, hundreds of readers have contacted me on my Web site, through call-in radio shows, and during my book-tour appearances with stories of their own unfinished business. I have included some of the most instructive and inspiring of these stories in this paperback edition of the book with the hope that you will continue to share your experiences, challenges, and the lessons you've learned with me and with other readers at www.myunfinishedbusiness.com.

To Wallow or Not to Wallow? That Is the Question

Cesar, a realtor from Los Gatos, California, had lost his business and home. But he was trying to rise above that trauma by reevaluating his life. "When you're faced with losing everything, you really have to dig down deep and say, 'Wow, who was I, who am I, and where am I going,'" he explained when he called into NPR's *Talk of the Nation* show while I was being interviewed.

Cesar could have chosen to wallow in despair when his world fell apart. Instead, he took stock of his life and concluded that "I wasn't very happy with the person I had become. So I started changing spiritually, and I decided to go back and say to people: 'I'm sorry,' 'I love you,' and 'Let's be friends again and pick up where we left off.'" By reaching out and reconnecting with people, Cesar strengthened his relationships, his support network, and his self-confidence.

"I Think He Would Really Want to Meet You."

Jeff hadn't spoken to his father in nearly eight years. ("My dad's an alcoholic," he explained. "He didn't show up at our wedding.") But Jeff's heart had begun to soften: "I found out through my mom that apparently he's got some health problems with his kidneys, and it looks like he has hepatitis. I'm not really angry with him. I'm more hurt and perplexed that he wouldn't want to connect with me. I think there's a lot of fear on his part and a lot of hurt on mine, and I think one of the best ways that I can reconnect with him is . . . I think he would really want to meet his granddaughter."

"I Was Told I Wasn't Good Enough for Him."

"Thirty-nine years ago, my fiancé drowned. I had been very close to his parents, especially his mother," H. C. wrote. "The minister told them to take a vacation and I thought it strange that they didn't talk to me before leaving. I was told they no longer wanted to see me; that my presence, at church and in their home, would be too painful for them. I was also told I wasn't good enough for their son, which is why God took him away! Not wanting to cause them any more pain, I moved away without another word to them.

"At fifty-eight, I made a trip back for a class reunion," she continued. "Then I decided to relocate here. My fiancé's mother is now in a care center. Once I worked up the courage to do so, I visited her. The immediate response of hugs and tears proved to me that she never told me to stay away! Her love, gentleness, kindness, and acceptance of me, all these years later, have healed so many old wounds!"

Happy Birthday

"I had lost contact with a friend from back in high school," wrote AceyLacey. "We had always wished each other 'Happy Birthday' on our birthdays. This year, as it was my fiftieth birthday, I picked up the phone to wish my friend a happy birthday as well. I was pleasantly surprised to hear her voice on the other end of the phone. We cried some, and have not stopped talking since."

Happy Birthday II

It had been several years since Sean had talked to his jazz musician father, who lived three thousand miles away in New Hampshire. Sean had just learned that his dad's favorite club was being torn down. "So I'm booking a flight from San Francisco to Portsmouth," he told me and the NPR radio audience. "I'll be there for his last show. It just so happens that it's going to be on his birthday. I want to record him playing as a keepsake."

The Healing Power of Never Too Late

TJoyce wrote: "When I was in second grade the lady who had been our music teacher died after a long bout with cancer. Her daughter Mary was a classmate of ours. Adults told us not to think or talk about it. We were not supposed to feel sorry for Mary and to let her get right back to schoolwork."

Years later, TJoyce saw Mary's name on a classmate reunion site. "I immediately contacted Mary to tell her how much we all liked her mother and how bad I felt all these years. Mary wrote back and said she was very grateful, as she had not known about the 'gag order' and she had always thought that nobody cared. *We* cared. It took over forty years, but Mary and I now have a friendship that I do not truly deserve, except for the healing power of never too late."

Just Do It!

Howard Sculthorpe, a retired engineering manager, wrote how he had lost touch with his Uncle Tony, who wasn't really his uncle, but who had played hide-and-seek with him and his two older sisters when he was a child and had served as a kind of surrogate dad. "Then something in the relationship went sour—a grown-up issue, which was not discussed with the kids. We went on with our lives, growing up, going to college, getting married, and so on. We lost track of Uncle Tony."

Howard had been wondering about Uncle Tony for years. Then one afternoon, as he and his wife were driving along the Brooklyn-Queens Expressway, he wondered aloud how Tony might be faring. "We concluded that it would only take an hour or two to find out, so we looked him up in the Brooklyn phone book and called. His sister answered and said he had been very ill. We wended our way through the Brooklyn streets to his home. He had suffered badly from a blood condition, which had recently cost him his leg. He was delighted to see us. He seemed to take special pleasure seeing how the young boy he had known for so long turned out, now with his own family. It was clear that we had made his day."

Uncle Tony died two weeks later. "It would have taken only the merest hesitation on my part to say: 'Forget it. Too much water has flowed over the dam—it's too late to reestablish relationships so long neglected. It would have been just as easy to rationalize postponing a visit or giving up on someone if he wasn't home. What a loss that would have been for me!" Howard wrote. The lesson he had learned? "Just do it!"

Sibling Reunion

"My sister and I had a very bad falling-out seven years ago," Rezza wrote. "We said horrible words to one another and she said she never wanted to hear from me again. Then our mom passed away. I stayed up many a night crying my heart out. My heart was breaking because I didn't have my sister, my only sibling, to talk to.

"Several months ago I finally got up the nerve to call her. I figured the worst that could happen was she would hang up on me. She didn't. When she picked up the phone, she told me how badly she had wanted to talk with me when our mom died but she had been afraid to call me. We talked for hours that night.

"Last month, my husband and I flew to Florida to see her. It was such a wonderful reunion and all the bad things we had said to one another were forgotten. We hugged, cried, and hugged some more. It's been over a month since we saw each other but we talk every night and I can't wait until I see her again in January. I am so happy I got up the nerve to call her. Life is too short to say and do bad things to each other."

"Life Had Taken Us Away from Each Other."

Mohana Narayanan wrote: "I am a sandwich child between two sisters and grew up with the usual middle-child syndrome: the peacemaker, the negotiator, forever striving to catch up with the elder sister, competing with the younger one for attention, and striving to keep ahead.

"Life was full of compromises, and there came a time when I kept away from home to escape the turmoil of personality clashes, with the parents taking obvious sides. All three of us married and moved, and somehow the angst that my elder sister carried against me became full-blown. I guess it was also because I was successful professionally and she was not; I realized in retrospect that my time away from home gave me the opportunity to hone my skills and I had to thank her for it!

"Life took us further and further away from each other, and years passed by with the disconnect growing, and also the chasm widening with unfinished and unresolved conflicts.

"I became a counselor; it opened up a lot of avenues for me. My personal growth was tremendous, but my emotional closure on a lot of issues made me visit my sister when I visited her city last year. Just no reason; just called up and told her I would like to come and see her. I don't know if she was taken aback; if she was she did not show it. There was awkwardness in our first meeting after almost four years, but I sensed warmth. We did not speak of issues—there were not any to speak of—but when I left I told her I was happy to reconnect, and I thought I detected a tear in her eye.

"About six months later, we had a sudden financial crisis; my husband was out of a job and suddenly the burden I had been bearing for the last five years, of running the family practically single-handedly, became too much for me to handle. I reached out to her. Just wrote to her saying I needed help; I did not specify what kind of help, just said I was tired. She did not mail me; she picked up the phone and called and just said 'Sit back, I am here, we will handle issues, not to worry.'

"The way things turned out was all secondary. The way she and her family pitched in would need another e-mail, but the connect I felt a year back had nothing to do with her coming back to my life as my savior now, for the connect was what I wanted. The phone call she made on her own was something that sealed the connect.

"I did not let go of issues: There was nothing to let go; but I realized that this unfinished business was something I am so glad I completed during that visit to her place."

"I Got to Tell Her That I Loved Her."

"My mother died when I was six; my dad remarried when I was thirteen or fourteen. I was the typical stepson: a brat and a punk, self-centered, and just a jerk. I showed my stepmother no respect." Then "Mugger," as he called himself, had a change of heart. "I joined the Navy at seventeen to get away from home. As I grew older, and maybe because of the Navy, I realized that my step-mother was a wonderful woman. The thing I am most thankful for is that I got to see her a few times before her death to let her know how much I cherished my time with her; I got to tell her I loved her. Thank God for that!"

You Know We've Got to Find a Way/ To Bring Some Loving Here Today

"I came from a home with an older brother who was on drugs for most his life," Twanna wrote. "It cost my parents their marriage. I had a failed marriage myself, with one child. I left home for my safety and to keep my child safe from my brother, so he would never be alone with her.

"One Thanksgiving holiday I thought we could be together again—what a mistake. My brother was back on drugs and abusive towards us. The holiday dinner was ruined. I vowed never to see him again. He ended up in jail for a year. I saw the strain on my parents.

"When my brother got out he looked great. I invited him to my home, but was careful. I decided to forgive him and move on. I needed to make things right for the sake of the family. For that I will be forever grateful. That Christmas we talked for the longest time and found peace. He died of a drug overdose two months later. He left knowing I cared."

One Step at a Time

"After years of alcoholism and drug abuse, I turned my life over to a 12-step program," Czarmommy wrote: "I am 19 years, 10 months, 28 days clean and sober.

"I started small: calling a local car dealer 'Mr.' despite his insistence I call him Pat. I'd abused so many people, it was now my privilege to show them the respect they deserved. I went on to bigger things like returning items I'd 'borrowed' only never returned, then to money. My older brother had lent me three thousand dollars at one time. I never paid it back, and it was the elephant in the room for me. At thirteen years sober I did so (with interest). No more elephants!

"Going through some old picture albums, I found pictures of my ex-husband and his family, looked him up, and sent them to him, thirty years later, with a note wishing his life has been well. Now, I'm searching for an ex-boyfriend to right a wrong, lifting another burden, setting me free."

Call Me "Insufferable."

"I had no idea how deeply a sixteen-year-long abusive marriage had affected my life and relationships, even long after I left it," wrote SpringSnow.

"My unaddressed PTSD (post traumatic stress disorder) exacerbated years after the fact, and I realized how many people I'd hurt for years with my defensiveness and fear. I called former co-workers, bosses, acquaintances, and relatives, apologizing for what I'd put them through and opening up about my illness. Nearly all of them had an 'aha' moment of understanding when I spoke of the PTSD. Most were understanding and forgiving. A couple of people were unable to let go of their anger toward me, and I decided to just put them on my prayer list. But by far the most poignant encounter was with a former co-worker who'd just been diagnosed with terminal cancer. While she heartily agreed I'd been insufferable, it was humbling to have reached out to her in time and heal some of the hurt I'd caused."

The Importance of Being Kind

Uma Girish wrote: "My deepest and best friendships have also been my worst emotional triggers. I had a friend (we'll call her Nan) who always called me when she was in the middle of an emotional crisis or needed a shoulder to cry on. When life was going well, I was usually forgotten. Or that's how I felt. And we lived right next door to each other. This up-and-down continued; we talked about it, she promised to mend her ways, I forgave her, we restarted and then the same story repeated itself. It got to a point when I told myself I couldn't take it any more. I cut the friendship. I stopped calling her. I wanted to have nothing to do with her.

"Then life threw us a surprise . . . after an entire lifetime of living in India, my husband and I decided to move to Chicago with our daughter. I did not call Nan, or convey the news to her. She was officially out of my life. A few days before we were due to leave, Nan and I crossed each other's paths. I walked on one side of the road, she on the other, each ignoring the other. When I got home I felt really bad about what had just happened so I picked up the phone and told her we were leaving. All she said was: 'Good luck. Have a good time.' We hung up.

"One month after I moved, my mom was diagnosed with stage four breast cancer. Eight months later, she died. That left a huge hole in my life and a heck of a lot of existential angst. I suddenly woke up to the fact that life is precious and that we need to take this journey with compassion, kindness, and love for all . . . for that's all we leave behind. I wrote Nan a long e-mail, owning up for my part in the whole drama and apologizing. She wrote back telling me how angry she truly was with me and how she hated me for giving up on her. I continued the correspondence with kind words, forgiving words, and we renewed our relationship.

"I traveled to India this summer and made it a point to meet her. We'd made big plans to catch up and lunch together but unfortunately all we got was an hour. My dad took ill and passed away on August 8 while I was on vacation. I'm so glad we had that one hour. We rediscovered the threads that bound us together and made a fresh start for what I've promised myself will be the friendship of a lifetime."

"It Just Felt Like Such a Tragedy to Me."

When Katie, a musician from Iowa City, didn't have enough money to finish recording an album, she asked her friends and family to pre-order it. "Then I discovered that one of the hard drives had been lost and I wasn't actually going to be able to finish the album. And I kind of just left it there, and I didn't ever really let these people know that they weren't going to get this album and that I wasn't going to finish it. It just felt like such a tragedy to me."

Katie had just made another album when she called in to share her story on *Talk of the Nation*. "I'm going to track down that list of people and send them this album instead," she said. "It's not the same music but it's, you know, it's from the same source, and hopefully they'll understand."

Up, Up, and Away

Several readers have noted how difficult it is for them to make amends to someone who is too infirm to comprehend their gesture. One reader, who identified himself only as "a recovering alcoholic/addict," came up with a particularly effective and touching solution for reaching out to his father, who had Alzheimer's. "I cannot make direct amends to him," he wrote. "So I have written him a letter apologizing for my past behavior and the hurt that I caused him. And on Father's Day, I will attach the letter to a balloon and let it go into the sky. This will be my tribute to him."

Sometimes It's Better to Let Sleeping Dogs Lie

Of course there are some amends it's better not to make. A sixty-three-year-old reader who referred to himself as "Troubled" wrote how he had wronged his first girlfriend when he was nineteen. A few years earlier, he had sent her a certified letter telling her how sorry he was. "It was signed for by her husband," he said. "I have no idea if she ever read it. My health is not good now. I do not want to die without being able to tell her how sorry I am. What do I do now?"

I advised him to leave her alone. "The point of telling her that you're sorry is to bring a measure of peace to her life. But if you try to contact her again, you risk creating doubts and tension in her marriage, something contrary to your goal of making amends. My guess is she really does know how sorry you are. Even more importantly— *you* know. This should help to ease your mind and conscience."

"The Weight Lifted from My Spirit."

Hyclean shared the following story: "Nearly twenty years ago, while serving a church, the church endured a tremendous upheaval, during which time it nearly destroyed itself in its emotional reactivity. I was personally hurt and a mean-spirited, vindictive, and spiteful superior damaged my career. I held resentment for years, not only for what he had done to me, but for his peers and colleagues who had protected his vicious lying, and who did not hold him accountable.

"I had no recourse. I was eventually vindicated for what he had accused me of, but by that time it was too late, and he never apologized. I was unable to forgive him, despite my mother's encouragement, until one day, it hit me that I was ready to do it and knew how I was going to do it. The next week, I arrived at his church for early Easter services and after the service he greeted me at the door, acting as though he was pleased to see me.

"When he put out his hand, I slipped an envelope into it; inside was a note that read, 'I have now forgiven you and am able to wish you well.' I slipped out and the weight lifted from my spirit. I never heard from him, so I don't know what he thought of my note, or if he even read it. Of course that doesn't matter, because the forgiveness was for me, not for him."

"I Feel Like I Just Won the Lottery."

At the writer's request, I have changed several names in this highly personal account of her pregnancy and her son's disease.

" 'ONE THOUSAND.'

" 'One thousand dollars?' Sid asked. With that dollar amount, I had gained my husband's full attention.

" 'She helped us when there was no one,' I explained. 'I'm not sure I would have made it without her.'

"My husband didn't say a word. He just looked at me with eyes that remembered the pain."

"SID AND I had known each other for just a few months. Our life had been full of parties and friends. Then everything changed. I got pregnant.

"Pressured by family, we got married at town hall. I wore a black maternity gown to the ceremony. There were no witnesses. The justice of the peace had the grace not to glance down at my protruding stomach. That night, Sid and I drove into town to celebrate. As we were walking from the car to the restaurant, my contractions began.

"Steven, the love of my life, was born healthy and beautiful. But a few months later his skin, from head to toe, turned an angry red. At the supermarket strangers would stare at him. Mothers would pull their children away, afraid that they would catch my son's 'disease.'

"The doctors told us that they had never seen such a severe case of eczema. Steven's body, fighting unknown allergens, succumbed to infection after infection and fever after fever. The medications the doctors gave him did nothing to ease his suffering. I felt powerless. My little baby was miserable and I couldn't make him well.

"Sid and I used up our money and credit flying Steven to specialists in other cities. Staying in cheap hotels, we'd take turns holding Steven as he cried through the night. During the day I'd hold and try to calm him as the nurses took yet another sample of blood from his tiny leg. Meanwhile, the creditors were calling. All I could afford to eat during the day was a blueberry muffin. I would eat enough dinner to make sure that I could breast-feed my son.

"Because my relationship with my disapproving parents was terrible . . . because my friends were busy with their lives . . . because my husband's way of dealing with the stress at home was to stay late at the office, I had no one, absolutely no one. Except Jenny.

"When my friend John heard that I was pregnant, he asked his sister, who was moving into her parent's home, if she would rent her small condo to Sid and me. Jenny was thrilled that someone 'responsible' would be living in what had been her and her children's first home. She didn't have a lot of money, but she decided to charge us only enough rent to cover her mortgage.

"Jenny would call me from time to time to see how things were going. I would tell her how dizzy I was getting from the lack of sleep, how I kept getting into fender benders, how I was scared. She would listen to my problems and help me solve them. She told me to let Steven sleep in my bed; that way, I wouldn't need to make so many trips into his room at night and I would sleep better. This woman I hardly knew was what I needed most: a lifeline, a mom on the other side of the phone who could feel my worries and pain.

"And then, gradually, our money situation got even worse. I picked up the phone one day and called Jenny. 'I need to ask if you could lower the rent for us.' I felt terrible asking her that, especially after she had asked only enough rent from us to pay her mortgage.

"Jenny was silent, but only for a moment. 'How about a hundred less a month? Will that help?'

"I knew that a hundred less a month would be a sacrifice for her. 'Thank you so mu—' I started to say. But she didn't let me finish.

'Tell me how Steven is.' "

"SID AND I glanced outside our bay window. Our seventeen-year-old son was playing soccer with his friends in the backyard of our home. As he dribbled past his friend Greg and made a goal, you would never believe that he had suffered so much in the first years of his life.

"When he was four, after years of medications and hospital visits and a very close brush with death, we discovered Steven had an allergy to latex. The medical establishment was just beginning to realize that allergies to their latex gloves were causing nurses to die of anaphylactic shock. No one had realized that the latex elastics in Steven's diapers and even the cuffs on his yellow dump-truck shirt were anathema to his body. When latex was removed from Steven's life, he healed and thrived.

"Sid looked outside the window again and then back at me. 'Okay. Let's send her a thousand dollars.'

"I spent an hour at the card store. None of the cards with pre-written words could convey the gratitude I felt in my heart. Finally I found a card I liked. On the cover it had a black-and-white photo of a single tulip growing in a field. It was a simple image but also a strong one. And I placed a check for a thousand dollars inside.

"I heard from John that Jenny used the money to go on a vacation to the Bahamas with some of her friends. She told John that she felt like she had just won the lottery.

"That's exactly how I feel when I look outside and see my beautiful, healthy son."

A Young Man's Father's Day Epiphany

I have been pleased, over these past few months, with how many e-mails I've received from readers in their twenties and early thirties. For them, the story of my extraordinary year of trying to do the right things is a cautionary tale that will help them weigh the challenges they'll face in balancing their families and careers.

"Three months ago something happened to me . . . I recognized that there is more to life than phone calls and e-mails, than calling recruits and worrying about the team. I stayed up all night thinking: Is this the career path I want?"

The letter came from a young man who identified himself as an assistant coach of one of the nation's top college swim teams. He was also a new parent and it bothered him that he was already making excuses for not attending the important events in his son's life: "Will my son score his first goal or touchdown and I'll have to hear about it over the phone?"

Why was this young man so urgently writing to me?

On the Saturday before Father's Day, when he was two thousand miles away from home and his son for a swim meet, he had walked into a bookstore and started browsing through a copy of this book. As he perused it, he came across a reference I had made to Mark 13:33: "Take heed, watch, for you know not when the time will come" (122).

Although this passage is typically interpreted as meaning the time for death, the young man saw it as meaning the time for the job that would enable him to become a more present and involved father. He would need to stay vigilant, he explained, because the right opportunity would present itself to him "when it is meant to happen."

I was moved to write him back: "Because you've been working so long, as an athlete and coach, at such a highly competitive level, it's only natural for you to be questioning your current career path as you embark on the demanding new adventure of parenting. The impressive thing is that you already recognize the importance of balancing work and family life."

This thoughtful young man seemed eons ahead of me and the vast majority of the mainly middle-aged people who had shared their unfinished business stories with me. Whatever path he chose—whether he ended up coaching at a major college or a local high school or pursuing an entirely different career—he was likely to create a harmonious blend of family, faith, and work. I found myself wishing him the happiest possible life, one free of regrets and unfinished business.

I AM GRATEFUL to the following media outlets for encouraging their readers, listeners, and viewers to share their unfinished business stories with me: *Reader's Digest, Psychology Today, USA Weekend*, NPR's *Talk of the Nation*, and AARP.org.

The *Unfinished Business* Toolkit

I do not consider myself a self-help expert. I'm a workaholic who improved his life by reaching out to others and making amends. I have assembled the strategies that worked best for me into this toolkit as a resource for people who want to take care of their unfinished business. I hope you find it useful.

Getting Started

Addressing your unfinished business is a five-step process. It involves:

1. Taking stock
2. Facing your fears
3. Reaching out
4. Making amends
5. Reflection and personal growth

Each of these five steps is important to the process. Unless you face your fears, it will be difficult for you to reach out to the person you've wronged. Unless you reach out to the person, you can't make amends.

It is through reflection that you learn the lessons that will help you refine your conscience and continue making a heartfelt commitment to acting in accordance with your most deeply held ideals.

I highly recommend that you keep a journal of your experience. Use it to explore your fears, map your journey, record what you learn, and celebrate the unexpected rewards that come with keeping your load lean. And please feel encouraged to share your story. It is by sharing our struggles and successes that we help ourselves and each other lead more complete and compassionate lives.

Taking Stock

The following lists and questions will help you identify the unfinished business in your life.

10 Big Questions
- Think of all your relationships—friends, relatives, rivals, teachers, coaches, ministers, rabbis, mentors, former teammates and classmates, co-workers and bosses, former spouses, girlfriends and boyfriends, crushes, children. Are any of these relationships particularly tense or unresolved?
- Have you lost touch with someone who had once been important to you? Would you like to reconnect with that person?
- Is there a person you have trouble forgiving?
- Is there a person who torments your psyche or plagues your dreams? Do you find yourself wishing that this person would fail, get hurt, or even die?
- Is there someone you worry about—or wonder about—who you haven't seen in years?
- Does something or someone make you feel ignored, misunderstood, unappreciated, wronged, or invisible?
- Is there a person you wronged in some major or minor way who died before you could make amends?
- Is there anyone who died without knowing how much he or she meant to you?

- Is there an important task you keep putting off because it seems too difficult and time-consuming to complete?
- Is there something you find yourself doing or not doing that seems entirely opposed to your core values or the person you'd like to be?

20 Common Wrongs
(where applicable, check off and fill in the blanks)

_____ I took unfair advantage of _____

_____ I snubbed _____

_____ I insulted _____

_____ I betrayed _____

_____ I stabbed _____ in the back

_____ I nursed a grudge against _____

_____ I embarrassed _____

_____ I humiliated _____

_____ I spread false rumors about _____

_____ I undermined _____'s project or goals

_____ I turned away from _____ when he or she was in need

_____ I broke a promise to _____

_____ I lied to _____

_____ I stole from _____

_____ I bullied _____

_____ I was unkind to _____

_____ I cheated on _____

_____ I disappointed _____

_____ I ignored _____

_____ I spoke harshly to _____

10 Common Neglects
(check the categories that nag at you the most, then specify to whom, what, and why)

I neglected to . . .

_____ do what I said I'd do
_____ pay back a debt
_____ express the love or gratitude I felt
_____ attend my friend's wedding
_____ attend my relative's funeral
_____ help a friend in need
_____ stand up for someone who was wronged
_____ reciprocate a kindness
_____ answer an important phone call or e-mail
_____ stay in touch

7 Common "Should Haves"
- I should have been a better _____ (son, daughter, husband, wife, father, mother, partner, friend)
- I should have told _____ what he or she meant to me
- I should have kept my promise to _____
- I should have listened more attentively to _____
- I should have been there when _____ needed me
- I should have been less _____ (proud, disrespectful, greedy, self-serving, vindictive)
- I should have been more _____ (generous, giving, caring, courageous, humble, forgiving)

Facing Your Fears

This list will help you identify the fears at the root of your unfinished business.

I was afraid of . . .
. . . hurting someone's feelings
. . . losing money
. . . being embarrassed
. . . getting hurt
. . . not living up to someone's expectations
. . . succeeding
. . . failing
. . . becoming overcommitted
. . . damaging my reputation
. . . not being liked

I was afraid of . . .
. . . not having enough time or energy
. . . learning the truth
. . . intruding on someone's privacy/time/grief
. . . encountering painful memories
. . . doing something wrong/insensitive/inappropriate
. . . being seen as weak or soft
. . . adding to someone's misery
. . . not being remembered
. . . being perceived as having been a selfish person
. . . confronting a new or uncomfortable situation
. . . being exposed as a failure or fraud

I was afraid of . . .
. . . taking a risk
. . . upsetting the status quo

. . . letting someone down
. . . losing my edge
. . . seeming stupid/trivial/silly
. . . making someone sad or depressed
. . . reawakening old or inappropriate desires
. . . provoking a confrontation with someone
. . . losing someone or something I valued
. . . not living up to my promise or abilities
. . . something bad happening to me or a loved one

Reaching Out

It is easier than ever to locate and reconnect with people. You can find almost anyone in the world by using a combination of search engines and social networking sites. As you search for them on the Web, one old friend will lead to another and you'll begin to piece together a picture of their lives. In most cases, people will be happy and interested to hear from you. Still, observe common-sense etiquette when reaching out to people and be respectful of their privacy, current life circumstances, and time.

Some resources that might help:

Facebook (www.facebook.com)
Facebook is a social networking site that connects people with friends and others who work, study, and live around them. You can search for distant relatives, old classmates, and long lost friends who may have profiles.

LinkedIn (www.linkedin.com)
Also a social networking site, but business-oriented. You can use it to find former colleagues and friends.

Google, Yahoo, Bing
These are popular search engines. The right search can help you locate bios, phone numbers, and addresses.

Classmates.com
Find a friend or high school alumni from more than forty million members in over two hundred thousand affiliations. Please note that this is a paid membership. You may also be able to find your friends and former classmates on your high school and college Web sites.

Genealogy.com
Discover and preserve your family's unique story.

Ancestry.com
Discover your ancestors with the world's largest family history Web site. Start a family tree, browse census records, and more.

TheRememberingSite.org
More than a thousand questions in forty-four categories help you remember the past and write your family's story, or your own, then share it with others. Please note that there's a one-time registration fee.

Making Amends

Making amends is a four-part process. It involves:

1. Accepting responsibility for what you have done
2. Apologizing to the person(s) you have hurt or offended
3. Trying to reverse the effects of your mistake
4. Making a commitment that you will never repeat the offending or hurtful behavior

Making amends is not about confessing your sins or spilling your guts or making sure that the person you've hurt is aware of your pain. It's about repairing the pain you've caused another human being.

Sincerity is everything.

"I am sorry." "I was wrong." "Thank you." These phrases only have value if they come straight from the heart, without any expectation that you'll get anything in return, including the other person's forgiveness.

Your goal in making amends is to restore a sense of balance and mutual respect to your relationship.

That means listening more than speaking and putting yourself in the other person's shoes. It also means realizing that sometimes, just sometimes, it's best to let sleeping dogs lie.

I discuss in the prologue of the book how making amends is central to most religious traditions and to addiction-recovery programs. Because it involves painful memories and strong emotions, the process of making amends can get complicated. If you find yourself struggling with it or having doubts, seek the guidance of a trustworthy friend, therapist, or clergy member.

Reflection and Personal Growth

Once you embark on the journey of completing your unfinished business, you'll find yourself becoming more attuned to your fears and aspirations and to the growing array of words, sounds, sights, and behaviors that will inspire and motivate you to become a better and more connected human being.

Each new experience is an opportunity for reflection and personal growth. But where, in the rush of everyday life, can you find the time?

You have to make it.

I try to spend at least fifteen minutes a day writing about my unfinished business in my journal. I pay particular attention to what I felt and learned that day. The time you spend writing and reflecting on your experiences helps you become a more conscious, compassionate, and connected person.

Acknowledgments

David Black served this book ably as its agent and biggest cheerleader. Donna Jackson gave me wise suggestions that improved every chapter and my overall conception of the book. Anton Mueller brought out the book's inner rhythms through his intelligent, sensitive editing. I am indebted to all three for pushing me to explore the emotions that were hardest for me to face and for helping me achieve a narrative that speaks from the heart. I am also grateful to George Gibson, Sabrina Farber, Peter Miller, Carrie Majer, Kristina Jutzi, and Rachel Mannheimer at Bloomsbury; and to Antonella Iannarino, Joy Tutela, and David Larabell at the David Black Literary Agency.

Patricia Arnao, Dave Barger, Frances Cohen, Barbaralee Diamonstein-Spielvogel, Kate Edgar, Maria Eitel, Serena Fox, Bruce Frank, Terry and Robin Gilbert, Keith Hefner, Amy Hertz, Melanie Higgins, Bill Hoogterp, Jamie Kaplan, Kirk Kundtz, John Lebsack, Michelle Kydd Lee, Michael Lesy, Jim Nevin, Liz Perle, Steven Pressman, Wendy Puriefoy, Hedy Rapeport, Isadore Rosenfeld, Mark Roth, Robert Sachs, Richard Tait, Don and Amy of the Wild Hive Café, and Mary Woolley gave me encouragement when I needed it most. I am grateful to them for their insights and support.

Muse, adviser, mother of my children, architect of my life, insightful first reader, best friend, my wife Elizabeth deserves the deepest thanks . . . for giving me the family I always wanted and for her steadfast love.

Visit www.myunfinishedbusiness.com to get tips on addressing your own unfinished business and to share your personal stories with the author and others.

A NOTE ON THE AUTHOR

Lee Kravitz grew up in Cleveland, Ohio. He attended Yale and Columbia universities. An award-winning journalist, he most recently was editor in chief of *Parade* magazine. He lives in New York City and Clinton Corners, New York, with his wife and three children.